Giulia Poggiali

The book of
TUSCAN *cuisine*
traditional family recipes, collected around Tuscany

Cençio's Tripe

Today I'm going
to prepare:
- Florentine tripe
- tomato soup
- lampredotto in zimino
- lampredotto sandwiches
- pork cheek stew
and I've got some good
Montepulciano, too!

EcoLIBRI

First Published
by Arsenale Editore

Texts and recipes
Giulia Poggiali

Illustrations
Antonella Scolari - Laura Toffaletti

English translation
Laura Meneghetti

The book of Tuscan cuisine

1st Edition March 2010
© Ecolibri 2010

via Ca' Nova Zampieri, 29
37057 San Giovanni Lupatoto (Verona)

www.ecolibri.eu

Introduction

Tuscan cooking is characterised by simple elements and recurrent ingredients, which belong to an ancient and peasant past, when cooking used to follow the rhythm of seasons and harvests. That is why so many recipes are available, all of them involving such a great number of different ingredients. The most important periods of an year were the olive picking season, at the beginning of November, the pig slaughtering in December, the chestnut picking and, of course, the grape harvest between September and October.

Olive oil is widely used in all Tuscan recipes. It replaces butter and lard. Tuscan people pick olives by hand, when the fruits are still on the trees. This oil has particular features: green colour and a sort of spicy flavour, called "pizzichino" (spicy). Many dishes, such as fettunta or boiled cannellini beans, are linked with the olive harvest, as they help appreciate the quality of the new oil.

Beside olive oil, Tuscan cooking shows us other precious ingredients, such as Tuscan unsalted bread. This characteristic makes it the perfect accompaniment for some other palatable Tuscan specialities, like dry-cured ham, which is a salty and long-seasoned ham. Bread is also a common ingredient in Tuscan recipes. In the past, it was baked just once a week in wood-fed ovens. When bread was stale at the end of a week, people used to wet it with broth: that is how some excellent bread-based Tuscan dishes were born. Bread soup ("ribollita") and tomato soup ("panzanella") are just a few examples. Tuscan bread could also be placed in fish sauces, our "guazzetti", stuffed with boiled vegetables, such as black cabbage, or be transformed into a good dessert just by adding some raisin (grape bread) or rosemary (rosemary Easter bread).

Tuscan people are also called "mangiafagioli" (bean eaters) as beans are widespread in Tuscan recipes. Several kinds of beans are available in Tuscany, but certainly cannellini beans are the most well-known type. Nowadays, other forgotten kinds of bean are being reintroduced in Tuscan farming. Different areas of Tuscany produce a wide range of beans: zolfino bean in Pratomagno, Sorana bean IGP, San Michele white bean, piattella bean in Pisa, tondino bean in Cetica and Garfagnana bean.. Beans can be dressed with olive oil and salt and they represent the perfect side dish for many Tuscan recipes, such as T-bone steak.

In the Appenini mountains, chestnuts have been the primary ingredient of local cooking for very many centuries. During hard times, chestnut was the only type of food available. Chestnut flour replaced wheat flour in those areas in the past and it was used to prepare lasagne, polenta, and fritters accompanied by ricotta cheese or by other types of cheese. Today, people appreciate this fruit again (that is shown by its increasing price), so the ancient unforgotten chestnut-based recipes are back on our table.

As far as meat is concerned, pork and beef are the main ingredients of our main courses. As everybody knows, the T-bone steak is a symbol of Tuscan cooking all over the world. It is a chianina cow meat cut. The name of the cow derives from the valley where cattle is bred, that is Valdichiana. We also exploit other parts of a chianina cow, like, for example, the first three chambers of the stomach. The stomach, whose culinary name is tripe, is very popular, especially in Florence, where "trippai" (tripe sellers") serve tripe sandwiches. At lunchtime, their stalls are crowded with people who order tripe in zimino in summer or a broth-dipped Lampredotto sandwich in winter. They also sell Florentine tripe, pork cheek stew, tomato soup, ribollita and many other delicious specialities.

Pig slaughtering used to take place at the end of every year. A common proverb tells us that no part of a pig goes to waste. The Tuscan swine breed has a two-coloured skin and can be found mainly in the areas around Siena, to the north of Florence and to the south of Grosseto. The breed is particularly suitable for producing dry-cured ham and other typed of salted pork.

Pig-blood fritters, our "roventini", were the first type of food made from pigs. Salted roventini were prepared with flour and parmigiano cheese, whilst sweet roventini were prepared with eggs, candied fruits, sugar and cinnamon. The range of salted pork includes buristo, made with blood and fat, biroldo, made using head, entrails and spices, dry-cured ham, a delicious and salty variety of ham, rigatino, finocchiona, Colonnata lard, seasoned in marble tank, and soppressata.

Tuscan cooking also includes fish recipes. Crustacean and mussels are among the main ingredients of those dishes, especially on the coast. Arselle, mussels, razor clams, baby clams, cuttlefish, shrimps, mantis shrimps, crabs can be cooked in manifold ways, such as pasta, "in guazzetto", "in zimino", or in soups. Caciucco is the most famous soup on the Tuscan coast: it is a very simple dish that allowed to use unsold fish in a recent past. Fish was cooked with tomatoes and mussels, served with bread and accompanied by red wine.
Cheese made in the area of Siena and Casentino are different according to seasoning time and taste. They are the perfect ending of a Tuscan meal.

The most popular desserts are linked with our festivities. Florentine flatbread and cenci are Carnival desserts, rosemary bread and Lent biscuits can be found only at Easter and Saint Joseph's fritters are prepared on Saint Joseph's day. Other desserts belong to a specific season, when the main ingredient, such us grapes or chestnuts, are available.

Do not forget to accompany all these recipes with a good glass of wine, the essential element of Tuscan cooking. See the map to discover the most famous Tuscan wines.
Quantities given in this book are meant for four servings, except for biscuits, cakes, appetizers and main courses, which tend to be more abundant.

CONVERTIONS

1 in= 2,5 centimetre	1 lb= 450 grams	1 qt= 1,1 litre
1 oz= 28 grams	1 pt= 0,6 litre	1 gal= 4,5 litre

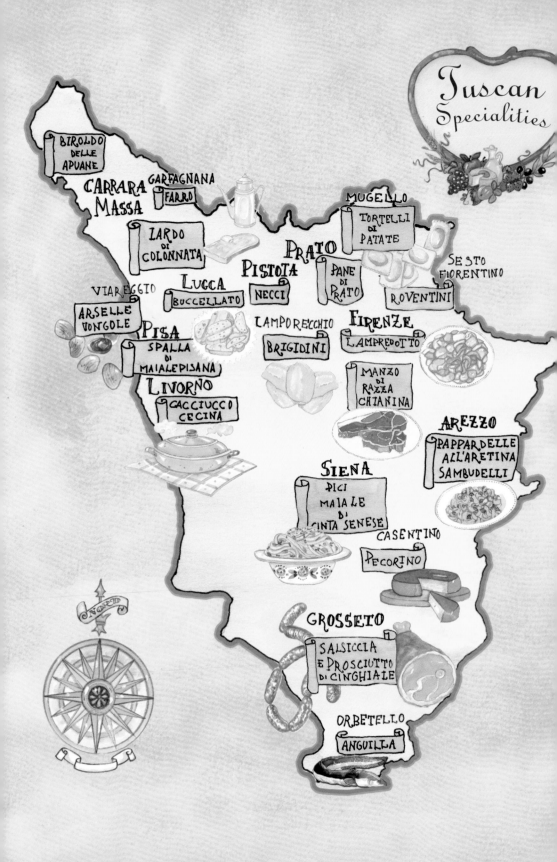

Tuscan Specialities

BIROLDO DELLE APUANE

CARRARA MASSA

GARFAGNANA FARRO

MUGELLO
TORTELLI DI PATATE

SESTO FIORENTINO

LARDO DI COLONNATA

PRATO

PISTOIA
PANE DI PRATO

ROVENTINI

VIAREGGIO

LUCCA
BUCCELLATO

NECCI

LAMPORECCHIO
BRIGIDINI

FIRENZE
LAMPREDOTTO

ARSELLE VONGOLE

PISA
SPALLA DI MAIALE PISANA

MANZO DI RAZZA CHIANINA

AREZZO
PAPPARDELLE ALL'ARETINA
SAMBUDELLI

LIVORNO
CACCIUCCO
CECINA

SIENA
PICI
MAIALE DI CINTA SENESE

CASENTINO
PECORINO

GROSSETO
SALSICCIA E PROSCIUTTO DI CINGHIALE

ORBETELLO
ANGUILLA

N

Indice

Appetizers and snacks.............................. 13
Black cabbage on toast 13
Chicken livers on toast 14
Coccoli... 15
Porcini mushrooms on polenta crostini 16
Arselle in the style of Livorno....................... 17
Fried sage.. 18
Sausage and stracchino cheese crostini 19
Prawn guazzetto 20
Bruschetta... 21
Guazzetto with mussels and clams.................. 22
Marinara mussels.................................... 23
Fettunta... 24
Necci 25
Cecina.. 26
Versiliese flat bread..................................28

First courses 29

'Gnudi 29
Tuscan pici pasta 30
Tuscan pici pasta with garlic-tomato sauce 31
Pici pasta with bread crumbs 32
Florentine crepes 33
Tortelli Mugellani 34
Pappardelle noodles in the style of Arezzo 36
Pappardelle with wild boar ragout 37
Spaghetti with favollo sauce 39
Florentine black risotto 40
Spaghetti with coltellacci sauce 41
Bavette pasta with red mullet 42
Risotto with cuttlefish 43
Spaghetti with mantis shrimps 44
Spaghetti with seafood sauce 45

Soups 47

Acquacotta: a Tuscan vegetable soup 47
Soup with pasta and beans 49
Bordatino soup 50
Spelt soup in the style of Lucca 51
Yellow porridge with Italian black cabbage ... 53
Garmugia in the style of Lucca 54
Carabaccia: a Tuscan onion soup 55

Lombardy soup...56
Fish soup..57
Caldaro in the style of Argentario.....................58
Arselle soup 59

Main courses...61
Stuffed chicken neck..61
Lampredotto in zimino.....................................62
Sheep stew..63
Florentine tripe..64
Recooked boiled meat with onions.....................66
Florentine marrowbones 67
Peposo in the style of Impruneta 68
Red mullets in the style of Livorno 70
Florentine steak..71
Chine of pork..72
Arrosto morto..74
Wild boar in the style of Maremma...................75
Roast wild boar 76
Spicy wild boar meat 77
Hare with dolceforte sauce...............................78
Etruscan-style rabbit.......................................80
Drunken octopus..81
Stuffed celery in the style of prato....................83
Florentine salt cod..84

Salt cod in zimino 85

Mantis shrimp stew 86

Bean in a fiasco 87

Scorpion fish in the style of Livorno 88

Stockfish with cards 89

Cuttlefish in zimino 90

Fagioli all' uccelletto 91

Peas in the Florentine style 92

Fried pumpkin flowers 93

Sauces and dips 94

Meat sauce 94

Fake ragout 95

Anchovy dip 96

Agresto sauce 97

Desserts 98

Anacini 98

Berlingozzo 99

Florentine carnival cake 100

Brigidini of Lamporecchio 101

Quaresimali 102

Ugly but good meringues 103

Rice fritters 104

Scarpaccia alla Viareggina 106

Buccellato 107

Schiacciata con l'uva 108

Castagnaccio 109

Cenci 111

Biscuits in the style of Prato 112

Gattò aretino 114

Rosemary bread 115

Ossi di morto 117

Ricciarelli 118

Zuccotto 119

Prato peaches 120

Rice cake in the style of Carrara 121

Liquor shots 123

Livorno punch 123

Florentine alkermes 125

Appetizers and snacks

Black cabbage on toast

*4 slices Tuscan bread, 4 bunches of black cabbage,
garlic, Tuscan extra virgin olive oil, salt*

This simple and tasty appetizer requires a typical Tuscan ingredient: the black cabbage. Boil the cabbage leaves in salted water. Toast the slices of bread, rub them with garlic and dip them quickly in the cabbage broth. Place each slice of bread in a bowl and lay some boiled cabbage leaves on it.
Dress with oil and some ground pepper.

CHICKEN LIVERS ON TOAST

1 onion, Tuscan extra virgin olive oil, 330 g chicken livers, a spoonful capers, fillets of achovy, a teaspoon butter, Tuscan bread, salt.

CAPPER

Brown a chopped onion in a saucepan. Clean and slice the chicken livers, add them to the onion and sprinkle with salt. Cook them over high heat for at least 15 minutes, stirring from time to time. Add half-glass of red wine progressively. Serve this dish with the same wine used for cooking the livers. Meanwhile, cook the anchovies with oil in a little saucepan until they dissolve. When the livers are cooked, chop them with capers and heat them again for a few minutes, adding anchovies and butter.

Slice bread and toast it. It should not be too thin. Spread each slice of bread with the livers and garnish with a caper.

These crostini are traditional Tuscan appetizers, usually served with many types of cold cuts and tomato on toast (bruschetta). This recipe belongs to my family tradition but changes can be made. For example, try chopping a raw anchovy with capers and cooked livers, or add chicken spleen to the livers, or brown an onion with a carrot and a few thin pieces of celery.

Coccoli

(Italian bread dough fritters)

300 g flour, 30 g yeast, 1 glass of water, salt, oil for frying

Coccoli are small fried salty bread dough fritters that have always been popular in Florence and all through Tuscany.

Dissolve the yeast in a glass of lukewarm water and pour it in a tiny well in the middle of the flour. Use a wooden pastry board. Add a pinch of salt and knead until you have a smooth dough. Place the ball of dough in a bowl dusted with flour, cover with a kitchen towel and allow leavening for 4-5 hours. After the dough has risen, divide the dough into small balls. Heat the frying oil and deep fry them for a couple of minutes.

You can still find some shops in Florence where Coccoli are served hot and salted, wrapped in yellow paper. Nowadays, Coccoli are served as appetizers in typical Tuscan trattorias and pizzerias, and in restaurants as well, together with ham and stracchino cheese.

Ficattole are quite similar to Coccoli, with some differences in the procedure. After the dough has risen, roll it out into a 0.5-cm-thick sheet. Cut out square shapes and deep fry them.

Porcini mushrooms on polenta crostini

300 g porcini mushrooms, slices of fried polenta*, some cloves garlic, olive oil, calamint leaves, leaves, salt, pepper.

Trim the roots of the mushrooms, and wipe away any dirt on the stems or caps. Rub them with a wet kitchen towel. Slice them, and sauté them over a brisk flame with chopped calamint leaves, oil, garlic, salt and pepper. When they have wilted and their water has evaporated, remove the garlic and place the porcini mushrooms on the slices of fried polenta.

* Cornmeal porridge

Arselle in the style of Livorno

1 kg arselle* (banded wedge shells), 1 onion, 1 clove garlic,
1 chilli pepper (to taste), 200 g tomato sauce,
4 slices bread, parsley, olive oil, salt, pepper.

Clean the arselle by soaking them in salted water for at least 12 hours; change the water frequently. It is advisable to use sea water in an earthenware vessel for this procedure, since arselle might die in a metal pot. After 12 hours, drain and let the arselle open by heating them over a brisk flame. As soon as they open, drain. Strain the arselle broth and eliminate all the empty shells. Meanwhile, sauté onion, garlic and the chilli pepper in a clean saucepan and then add the arselle. Dilute the tomato sauce with the arselle broth and pour it over the shellfish. Add salt and pepper to taste and cook over low heat for 20 minutes. Meanwhile, toast the bread and place each slice in a bowl. Pour the arselle sauce in the bowls and serve with fresh chopped parsley.

*Arselle might not be available outside italy. Arselle are definitely not vongole (striped venus clam) nor vongole veraci (chequered carpet shells): they're much smaller. If you cannot get hold of arselle, try the recipe with clams.

Fried sage

sage leaves, flour, 1 egg, salt, oil for frying

Fried sage can be served as an appetizer or to accompany the main course together with other fried vegetables. Select the biggest leaves, avoiding the hardest ones; rinse the leaves and trim off the stem. Mix the batter with the egg, flour and salt. According to your taste, you can decide whether you want to add a little water, milk or beer to make the batter foamy. Drop the leaves in the batter and deep fry them in oil for a few seconds, transferring them to paper towels to drain. Salt the leaves to taste.

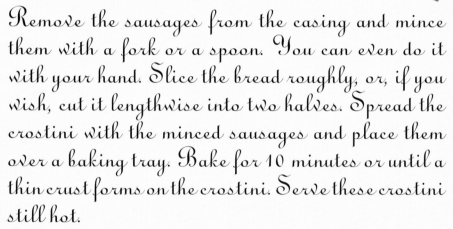

Sausage and stracchino cheese* crostini

3 fresh sausages, 150 g stracchino cheese, Tuscan bread

Remove the sausages from the casing and mince them with a fork or a spoon. You can even do it with your hand. Slice the bread roughly, or, if you wish, cut it lengthwise into two halves. Spread the crostini with the minced sausages and place them over a baking tray. Bake for 10 minutes or until a thin crust forms on the crostini. Serve these crostini still hot.

Another version of these crostini can be prepared with fennel seeds, that make the stuffing quite similar to the finocchiona, a type of Tuscan salami. Instead of stracchino cheese, you might also use raviggiolo cheese, which is saltier, but much more difficult to find in grocers' shops. Personally, I decorate these crostini with walnut kernels.

*Stracchino cheese is a soft, fresh, creamy cheese made from whole pasteurized cow's milk.

Prawn guazzetto

500 g prawns, garlic, parsley, white wine, half lemon,
cherry tomatoes, olive oil, chilli pepper powder, salt.

The prawn guazzetto can be served as appetizer or
as main course, together with slices of bread. You
can even toast the bread and place it in the soup
plates where you will pour the guazzetto. This recipe
belongs to a friend of mine from viareggio.
In a large pot pour half-glass olive oil, chopped
garlic, parsley and chilli pepper powder to taste.
Squeeze half-lemon and pour it in the pot together
with a glass of white wine and salt. If you want a
more fluid guazzetto add more wine. With a hand-
held immersion blender whisk the sauce and place
the prawn inside. Cover the pot and let it souse for
at least 4 hours, stirring from time to time.
Pour the prawn guazzetto in a large pan, cut the
cherry tomatoes in halves and add them to the
guazzetto. Cook for a few minutes, until the prawns
change their colour. Serve the guazzetto with the
slices of bread.

BRUSCHETTA

4 slices Tuscan bread, cloves of garlic, 4 ripe tomatoes,
4 leaves basil, olive oil, salt

Toasted and garlic-rubbed bread is the basis of every kind of bruschetta you might want to prepare, as it can be topped with whatever ingredient you prefer.

The most typical recipe includes a tomato topping; nevertheless a tomato bruschetta can be prepared in many different ways.

Broil the bread until it browns. Rub both sides of each slice with garlic. Clean, dry and cut into small pieces the tomatoes and then place them on each slice of bread. Pour a few drops of oil and salt to taste. Garnish with basil leaves.

Another type of tomato bruschetta can be prepared by marinating tomatoes, garlic and basil in oil with salt for an hour. Once soused, the topping can be placed on slices of broiled bread.

Guazzetto with mussels and clams

500 g mussels, 500 g clams, garlic, parsley, olive oil, salt, pepper, 4 slices homemade bread

Clean the clams by letting them in a bowl with salted water for about 6 hours. Clean the shells of the mussels. Allow clams to open by heating them in a pan with chopped garlic, parsley and pepper. Once the shells have opened, drain and keep the clam broth in a separate vessel; strain it if you think it might contain residues of sand or shells. In a pan, heat abundant olive oil with three chopped cloves of garlic and parsley. Pour clams and mussels in the pan and cook for 5 minutes. Add white wine, salt and pepper to taste. Place a slice of toasted bread in each soup plate and pour the guazzetto. Sprinkle with some parsley and some drops of oil.

Marinara mussels

1,5 kg mussels, 1 carrot, 1 onion, garlic, parsley, bay,
50 g butter, white wine, Tuscan bread, olive oil, salt, pepper

Clean the mussels with the help of a wire brush, removing all the growths by holding the mussel firmly between index and thumb and pulling towards the large side. Wash them thoroughly under running water. Slice the carrot and the onion and place them in a pan with olive oil, 2 cloves of garlic, a glass of white wine, some bay, butter, salt and pepper. Cook over brisk flame, stirring frequently. Add the mussels, heating them until the shells open. Place toasted bread on a tray. Remove the empty halves of the shells from the mussels and place the mussels on the bread. Strain the sauce and pour it on the tray, in order to cover all the slices. Serve with parsley and fresh-ground pepper.

Fettunta

This is a typical Tuscan appetizer and snack during the olive picking time. In Tuscany, olives are picked before they fall from the trees, and their green freshly squeezed oil is called "pizzichino". Olive pickers use this snack to taste their oil directly at the oil-mill. In order to taste this precious oil properly, Tuscan people toast slices of bread, rub them with garlic, wet the bread with oil and sprinkle with little salt. Fettunta is usually served warm.

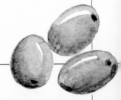

NECCI
(CHESTNUT-FLOUR CREPES)

350 chestnut flour, salt, waffle iron (or a 6-to-8-inch non-stick pan)

Necci are thick chestnut-
flour fritters.
They can be found all over
Tuscany, above all in the
Appenini mountains, near
Pistoia and in Garfagnana, where
wide chestnut woods grow spontaneously.
Prepare a batter with flour, water and salt, making sure
not to leave any lump. The batter must be smooth but not
too watery. Grease a pan or a waffle iron and pour enough
batter to cover the bottom evenly. Cook both sides of the
fritter until the it becomes firm and golden. Repeat the
process with the remaining batter. Necci should be no higher
than 1 cm. Serve hot. If you wish, fold necci in or roll them.
You can stuff them with ricotta cheese, stracchino cheese,
mascarpone cheese or pecorino cheese. Necci with sweet
stuffing can be served as a dessert or a snack, whilst necci
with salty stuffing can be an excellent appetizer.

Cecina

(chickpea flour flat bread)

350 g chickpea flour, water, salt, olive oil, pepper

Cecina is a sort of flat bread which is very popular along the Tuscan coast. The original recipe came from Liguria centuries ago and it spread through Tuscany, so receiving many different names. It is called farinata (made of flour) in Lunigiana, calda calda (hot hot) in Massa Carrara, cecina on the Versilia coast and in the town of Cecina, torta (pancake) in Livorno, where people eat it between two slices of bread. It was also called 5 e 5 (5 and 5) there, because a slice of cecina used to cost just 5 cents of an Italian lira, plus 5 cents for the bread. There are tortai (cecina bakers) in Livorno and Pisa who still cook this type of flat bread in wood-fed ovens, but cecina can be easily found in all

Tuscan bakeries and pizzerias. It can be prepared and eaten at any time of day.

Place the flour in a large bowl and slowly pour a litre of cold water over it. Add some salt and stir until the mixture becomes liquid, smooth, without lumps. Let it stand for a few hours. Remove any foam that forms at the top and stir again. Add three spoons of olive oil and stir. Pre-heat oven to 200° (400°f). Grease with oil a large, round pan with low borders. Add the mixture, making sure it is pretty low - the cecina has to be no higher than ½ cm (about ¼ inch) high, so if your pan is not wide enough to make it like this, bake separate batches. Bake in very hot oven for at least 40 minutes, until cecina has a golden crust at the top. Cecina must be soft in the middle and crisp on the outside. Grind a lot of fresh black pepper on top of the cecina as soon as it comes out of the oven.

Versiliese flat bread
(crisp olive and herb flat bread)

300 g cornmeal, 500 g flour (wholemeal flour, if possible),
dried yeast, 200 g black pitted olives, rosemary, sage leaves,
2 cloves garlic, olive oil, table salt, cooking salt

The name of this kind of flat bread refers to a section of the Tuscan coast, called Versilia. Nevertheless, this recipe is widespread on the whole Tuscan coast. Chop sage leaves, rosemary and the cloves of garlic. Mix both types of flour with some salt in a bowl. Allow yeast to reactivate by dissolving it in a bowl with warm water. The package itself might contain instructions about this process. Pour the yeast in the bowl with flour and salt and stir. Add two spoons of olive oil, pitted olives and herbs. If necessary, add water to make the dough be rather similar to bread dough. Roll out the dough on a pastry board and then place it in a 1 - cm baking tray or casseruole. Dimple the top of the dough with your fingertips and sprinkle with some extra salt and 2 teaspoons of oil. Bake in oven to 200° for 40 minutes. Serve warm or at room temperature.

First courses

'Gnudi

300 g ricotta cheese, 300 g spinach, 50 g grated parmigiano,
3 egg yolks, salt, flour, nutmeg.

The name 'Gnudi comes from the word "ignudi" (naked): this word refers to the traditional stuffing of ravioli, which is "naked" without the ravioli dough. Boil spinach in little salted water. Once they wilt, drain and squeeze them. Chop the spinach and place them in a bowl. Add ricotta, parmigiano and freshly grated nutmeg. Stir and add egg yolks. Knead the mixture with your hands and then form small balls.

Rub the dough balls with flour and cook them in boiling water. Once ready, remove them from the water with a slotted spoon. You can serve the 'Gnudi with butter and sage or with broth. It is advisable to sprinkle 'Gnudi with parmigiano. This recipe comes from the Casentino area - that is why 'Gnudi are also called "Casentino dumplings" - but it is widespread all through Tuscany.

Tuscan pici pasta

(fresh pasta)

350 g all-purpose flour, 1 glass of water, salt

Pici are a kind of fresh handmade spaghetti, who looks rough and thick. You can easily buy this type of pasta in pasta shops or even in bakeries in Siena and Grosseto. Mix all the flour with water and a pinch of salt and knead until the dough becomes rather firm. Let it stand for a quarter of an hour. Roll it out into a 0,5-cm-wide thick sheet on a pastry board. Cut the sheet of dough into 30-cm-long and 1-cm-wide strips. Sprinkle the strips with some flour and roll

each strip into a thick strand of spaghetti using your hands. Cook pici in boiling water for a few minutes. The perfect dressing for pici is meat ragout.
Once prepared with water and flour, today an egg is added to the pici dough.

Tuscan pici pasta with garlic-tomato sauce

4 large cloves garlic, 300 g fresh tomatoes, extra virgin olive oil, 400 g fresh pici, salt, pepper

Brown garlic with olive oil in a large saucepan over low heat. Garlic should not fry. Clean the tomatoes, remove all the seeds and cut them into cubes. Add tomatoes to the garlic and let the mixture cook for 10 minutes. Add a pinch of salt. Meanwhile, cook pici in salty water. A tablespoon of oil in the water will help you prevent pici from sticking together. Remove pasta from the pot using a slotted spoon and transfer it into the pan where the sauce is. Cook briefly, until pasta is coated. Sprinkle pasta with fresh-ground pepper and serve it.

Pici pasta with bread crumbs

3 cloves garlic, 2 slices Tuscan bread, extra virgin olive oil, salt, pepper, Tuscan pecorino cheese

Pour some olive oil into a pan and sauté three cloves of garlic. Broil two slices of Tuscan bread, place them in the pan and reduce the bread to crumbs. Add a pinch of salt. Meanwhile, cook pici pasta in boiling salted water with a tablespoon of olive oil. Drain and sauté pici pasta with the bread crumbs in the pan. Remove the cloves of garlic and sprinkle with pecorino cheese or parmigiano cheese. Serve with ground pepper to taste.

Florentine crepes

2 eggs, 200 g sheep's milk ricotta, 200 g cooked spinach,
100 g all purpose flour, 250 ml milk,
freshly grated parmigiano cheese, tomato sauce, pepper,
salt, a pinch freshly ground, nutmeg, 1 l béchamel

Prepare the crepe mixture with eggs, milk, flour and a pinch of salt. Stir the mixture, dissolving all the lumps. Pre-heat a small non-stick-20cm-pan. Make 8 thin firm and golden crepes.
Prepare the stuffing: mix minced spinach, ricotta and parmigiano cheese in a bowl. Add salt, pepper and nutmeg to taste. Place an amount of stuffing on each crepe and roll the crepes up.
Place half of the béchamel into a casserole and place the rolled crepes on it. Pour the remaining white sauce. Sprinkle with grated parmigiano cheese and pour some tablespoons tomato sauce on the surface. Bake the crepes over medium heat for 15 minutes.

Tortelli* Mugellani

Dough: 1 kg flour, 6 eggs, salt

Stuffing: 2 kg potatoes, parsley, garlic, tomato sauce,
grated parmigiano cheese, fresh ground nutmeg,
extra virgin olive oil, salt, pepper

This is a traditional recipe of the Tuscan area of Mugello, but it is also widespread in Prato and in the surroundings of Arezzo, especially in Casentino. It is easy to find tortelli in Tuscan typical restaurants, and festivals are held around Tuscany to celebrate tortelli both in Summer and in Autumn.

Boil the potatoes in salted water. While waiting for the potatoes to cook, place the flour on a board and add eggs and salt in a well in the middle of the flour. Knead the dough, adding lukewarm water gradually. The result should be a smooth and elastic dough. Let it stand for a while.

Drain the potatoes and mash them with a fork. Chop parsley and garlic, sauté them in a pan with olive oil. When garlic browns, add a glass of tomato sauce. Mix the mashed potatoes with the sauce and add a glass of parmigiano cheese, ground nutmeg to taste, salt and pepper. Stir and if you think the stuffing is too dry, add some olive oil.

Roll out the dough you have let stand and cut it into square 5-cm-wide shapes. It is advisable to use a pastry wheel. Place the stuffing on half of the dough shapes and cover tortelli with the shapes left. Close ravioli carefully, pressing delicately the edges with you fingers.

You might also prepare round tortelli by using a glass to cut out the sheet of dough. Place some stuffing in the middle and fold each tortello, pressing the edges with your fingers in order to close it.

Cook tortelli in boiling water for 4 minutes. Serve with mushroom dressing or meat sauce. Red wine is recommended to accompany this dish properly.

* type of ravioli

Pappardelle noodles*
in the style of Arezzo
(with nana sauce)

400 g fresh pappardelle pasta, 1 small domestic duck, 50 g bacon, 400 g pealed tomatoes, 1 carrot, 1 onion, 1 stalk celery, sage, red wine, olive oil, salt, pepper, parmigiano cheese

This is a typical winter dish from Arezzo and Siena. The small duck used for the ragout is called by Tuscan people "Nana" ("very small").
Clean the duck carefully and cut it into 4 parts. You might as well have the butcher chop it. Remove heart and liver and set aside them. Chop celery, carrot, onion and sauté the mixture in a large saucepan together with olive oil, some leaves of sage and bacon. As soon as the onion browns, place the duck in the saucepan and after a few minutes add a glass of red wine. Let the wine evaporate, season with salt and pepper to taste and pour peeled tomatoes onto the duck. Cover the sauce and cook for at least one

hour. Check the sauce from time to time to make sure if it is sufficiently liquid. Add broth or water if necessary. When the duck is ready, discard bones and skin from it, cut the meat together with heart and liver into small pieces and cook the mixture for one quarter of an hour. Meanwhile, cook pappardelle in boiling salted water. Drain and add the duck sauce. Sprinkle with parmigiano cheese. You might also prepare the duck as given in this recipe and serve it with its bones as a main course, accompanied by uccelletto beans, whilst the juice of the cooking duck can be added to pappardelle noodles with some pieces of liver.

*Pappardelle noodle are a type of Tuscan ribbon pasta, quite similar to fettuccine, but slightly larger.

Pappardelle with wild boar ragout

400 g fresh pappardelle noodles, 500 g wild boar, 500 g tomato sauce, 1 onion, parsley, red wine, olive, oil, salt

Place the wild boar meat in water for at least 12 hours before using it for this recipe. Change the water frequently, 4/5 times, until the meat does not release impurities anymore. Chop onion and parsley and sauté them with olive oil in a large saucepan. Reduce meat to small soft pieces and add it to the browned onion. Pour a glass of red wine onto the meat. A glass of Chianti would give the perfect taste to this sauce. Let alcohol evaporate and then add the tomato sauce, bay leaves and salt to taste. Cover and cook for about 3 hours, stirring occasionally. Add water if necessary. When the ragout is almost ready, it is time to prepare pappardelle noodles. Cook pappardelle in boiling salted water, drain and place them into the saucepan. Sauté pappardelle with the ragout and serve.

You might as well use this recipe for a wild boar stew. Cut the meat into large pie and cook it in a mixture of chopped onion, celery, carrot and olive oil. Do not add parsley to the stew.

SPAGHETTI WITH FAVOLLO* SAUCE

*Fish broth, 1 kg crabs, 1 onion,
3 cloves garlic, 1 chili pepper,
1kg peeled tomatoes, 350 g spaghetti,
olive oil, parsley, salt*

This is a traditional recipe from the Tuscan coast. Favollo is a large red crab, endowed with strong furry claws. Cook crabs in boiling fish broth for **20** minutes. You might as well cook them in vegetable broth. Meanwhile, sauté chopped onion and garlic in a saucepan with **8** tablespoons olive oil. Add chili pepper to taste. Drain crabs and break them into large rough pieces using a meat pounder. Pay attention to keep claws intact. Add to the fried ingredients both the crabs and the peeled tomatoes. Let the sauce cook without lid. Cook spaghetti in boiling salted water. Drain and transfer pasta into the pan, cooking it briefly until it is coated with sauce. Sprinkle with freshly chopped parsley and a little olive oil. If you wish to eat the crab meat, use a nutcracker.

* Favollo is the tipical Tuscan name for the warty crab

Florentine black risotto

400 g cuttlefish, 1 onion, 1 clove garlic, white wine, tomato sauce, 350 g rice, broth, olive oil, salt

Wash cuttlefish carefully. Remove the ink sacs, paying attention not to break them. Cut the cuttlefish into small pieces. Wilt a sliced onion in a saucepan with olive oil. Place cuttlefish in the saucepan, add half a glass of white wine, and let the alcohol evaporate. Add chopped garlic and tomato sauce, diluting it with water. Salt to taste. Let cuttlefish cook for half an hour. Prepare a fish broth or a vegetable broth. Add rice to the cuttlefish and pour some broth onto the mixture gradually, allowing cooking. A few minutes before the rice is ready, add the ink sacs. Stir and serve.

SPAGHETTI WITH COLTELLACCI SAUCE

500 g clean razor clams,
2 cloves garlic,
1 chilli pepper,
white wine,
200 g cherry tomatoes,
300 g spaghetti,
olive oil,
parsley, salt

This is a traditional recipe from Versilia, an area on the Tuscan coast, where the habit of collecting clams on the seashore after a night of stormy weather is widespread. People from Versilia call razor clams "cannolicchi" or "coltellacci". Open the razor clams, removing the shell. Clean and cut them. Brown garlic with olive oil in a pan, add chilli pepper to taste and place the razor clams into the pan. Wait for the water contained in the razor clams to evaporate. Add white wine and let the alcohol simmer and reduce. Cut cherry tomatoes into quarters and add them to the razor clams. Cook for at least 10 minutes. Cook spaghetti in boiling salted water till they are al dente. Drain and transfer spaghetti into the pan. Cook briefly over brisk flame until past is coated. Sprinkle with freshly chopped parsley and serve.

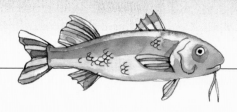

Bavette* pasta with red mullet

8 medium-size red mullets, 350 g bavette pasta, 2 cloves garlic, chilli pepper, parsley, oil, salt, pepper.

Clean the fish and cut it into fillets. Rinse the fillets with water. Brown garlic in a large saucepan with 6 tablespoons of oil. Add chilli pepper to taste. Place the fillets into the saucepan, paying attention not to break them. Add a glass of white wine and let the alcohol evaporate. Cook bavette pasta in boiling salted water. You might as well cook linguine or spaghetti instead. Drain and transfer bavette into the saucepan. Cook briefly. Sprinkle with chopped parsley and serve.

Another recipe for this dish could include a different procedure in cooking the red mullets. Remove the fish scale and cook the fish without cutting it. Pour a glass of wine on it and when the alcohol evaporates completely, remove head, tail and fishbone. Go on cooking, adding some fish broth from time to time. You can use tomato sauce instead of broth.

*Bavette pasta is quite similar to linguine.

Risotto with cuttlefish

400 g cuttlefish, 350 g rice, 2 cloves garlic, 1 onion, parsley, white
wine, fish broth, 40 g butter, olive oil, salt, pepper

Clean the cuttlefish removing the bone, eyes, beak
and entrails. Reserve the ink sacs without breaking
them. Pour 6 tablespoons of olive oil in a large
saucepan and brown chopped garlic, onion and
parsley. Add white wine and let it evaporate. Cut
the cuttlefish into small strips and place it into the
saucepan. Cover the saucepan with a lid and allow
cooking over low heat for one hour and a half.
Add rice to the sauce and stir carefully. Cook the
rice adding fish broth or vegetable broth. If you
wish, add the ink sacs a few minutes before the rice
cooks completely, stirring in order to give an even
black colour to the rice. Turn off the stove and add
butter to the rice. Wait until the butter melts. Stir
gently, sprinkle with fresh - ground
pepper and serve.

Spaghetti with mantis shrimps

700 g mantis shrimps, 4 cloves garlic, parsley, thyme, white wine, 350 g rice, olive oil, salt, pepper

Mantis shrimps are marine crustaceans called "canocchie" or "pannocchie" in Tuscany. Cut the thorns on the sides of the mantis shrimps and wash the fish. Boil mantis shrimps for 15 minutes in salted water. Add garlic, parsley, thyme and a glass of white wine. Allow the broth to cool and remove the mantis shrimps from it. Reserve set aside four intact mantis shrimps and cut the others in order to take out the meat. Chop some garlic and parsley and sauté this mixture in a saucepan together with some olive oil. Add the mantis shrimp meat and salt to taste. After seasoning the mantis shrimps in the saucepan, place the rice into it. Let it cook, pouring broth of mantis shrimps gradually. Serve rice into soup plates with a mantis shrimps on top. Sprinkle with parsley and fresh-ground pepper.

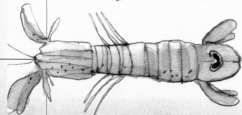

Spaghetti
with seafood sauce

400 g spaghetti, 300 g mussels, 300 g baby clams, 300 g squids,
8 shrimp scampi, 300 g cherry tomatoes, white wine, parsley,
garlic, olive oil, chilli pepper, salt, pepper

Clean mussels and baby clams by soaking them in salted water for 6 hours. Change the water at least three times in order to eliminate all the sand. Scrub the shells and let them open by cooking them in a pan over brisk flame. Strain the broth formed in the pan. Remove half the mussels and baby clams from their shells. Clean the squids and cook them in a separate saucepan with olive oil, chopped garlic, parsley and chilli pepper to taste. Cut tomatoes into halves and place them in the saucepan. Add half a glass of white wine and some of the broth formed by mussels and clams. Let it cook for 5 minutes. Add all the seafood and stir. Cook pasta in boiling salted water until it is al dente.

Drain and place spaghetti in the saucepan with the seafood. Stir and serve with parsley, fresh-ground pepper or chilli pepper.

Another version of this recipe includes a different procedure for the sauce. First, sauté baby clams in a saucepan with olive oil and garlic until they open. Add the mussels. As soon as they open, add squids and prawns scampi. Pour some white wine onto the sauce and when it evaporates, add cherry tomatoes.

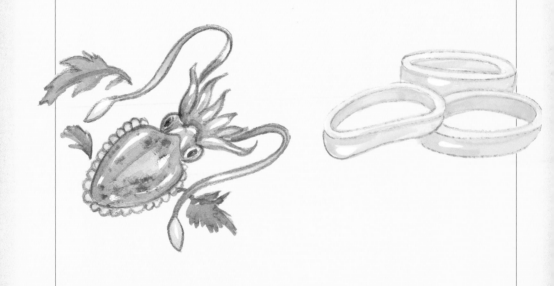

Soups

Acquacotta: a Tuscan vegetables soup

50 g extra virgin olive oil, 2 red onions, 1 stalk celery, basil, 4 ripe tomatoes, 4 eggs, 4 slices of homemade bread

Acquacotta was the typical dish of peasants and miners of Maremma, whose diet was particularly poor and based on vegetables and bread. Heat some olive oil in a pot and let chopped onions and the cloves of garlic wilt. Add tomatoes, roughly chopped celery, basil, salt, pepper and cook the mixture. Add a litre of water (or broth) and cook over medium heat for 15 minutes.

At this point, open the lid and break eggs on the surface of the soup without stirring, letting them set.

Place a slice of toasted bread into each bowl, sprinkle with pecorino cheese or parmigiano cheese, and pour Acquacotta into each bowl, paying attention to serve an egg in each bowl.

Acquacotta can be prepared in other ways, according to the area or the ingredients avaiable.

Aquacotta of Siena and Arezzo has mushrooms inside, since they are very easy to find around mount Amiata or in the woods of Casentino.

Aquacotta in the style of Casentino is prepared with sausage, whilst the peasants' Acquacotta is rich in vegetables, such as peas, chards, carrots, zucchinis and artichokes.

SOUP WITH PASTA AND BEANS

200 g small size pasta, 300 g dried cannellini
beans or 600 g fresh cannellini beans,
1 clove garlic, sage leaves,
rosemary, tomato sauce, olive, oil, salt, pepper

This soup with pasta and beans, also called "bean soup", is a typical Tuscan first course and it is widespread all over the region. If you decide to use dried beans, soak them in cold water for at least 12 hours. Boil the beans in 1.5 litre of salted water. Add a clove of garlic, two tablespoons of olive oil and some sage leaves, which must be removed when the beans are ready. Do not cook over high heat in order to make the beans cook properly without losing their peel. Once ready, remove just half of the beans, process it in a vegetable mills and place it into the pot again. Warm some olive oil with rosemary and tomato sauce in a saucepan. Tomato is used as a colouring not as a real ingredient. When olive oil is scented with rosemary, pour it into the pot of beans. Add pasta and salt to taste. Cook until pasta is ready. Let the soup stand a few minutes before serving it. Sprinkle with fresh-ground pepper and a few drops of olive oil.

This recipe belongs to my family, but manifold versions of it are possible. For example, cannellini beans could be replaced with borlotti beans, and chilli pepper and bacon can be added to them. Moreover, not only pasta could be used, but also rice or spelt.

Bordatino soup

200 g maize flour, 2 Tuscan black cabbages, 300 g kidney-beans,
tomato sauce, olive oil, 1 onion, 1 celery, 1 carrot, salt

Traditionally, this soup was the main food in the diet of the poorest people of Livorno. It was made with leftovers, in particular kidney-beans boiled the previous day, whilst black cabbage was added when available. This recipe has richer ingredients than the original Bordatino. Chop onion, celery, and carrot. Sauté them with olive oil in a saucepan. Add the tomato sauce, diluting it with water, and sliced black cabbage. Cook for 10 minutes. In another pot, cook the beans in boiling salted water. Drain and set aside a tablespoon of whole boiled beans and the broth. Mash the beans.

When the black cabbage starts to wilt, add both intact and mashed beans. Let the soup simmer. While the soup cooks, prepare a rather liquid polenta*. Five minutes before it is ready, pour it into the pot with the soup while stirring. Cook 5 more minutes. Serve with some drops of olive oil. You might as well add other ingredients to this basic recipe of Bordatino.

*Cornmeal porridge

Spelt soup in the style of Lucca

400 g dried borlotti beans, 2 cloves garlic, sage leaves, 1 red onion, 2 carrots, 1 stalk celery, 1 tablespoon tomato sauce, 2 slice bacon, 400 g Garfagnana spelt, extra virgin olive oil, salt, pepper

This is a rich soup prepared by people from Garfagnana, that is why it is also called "Garfagnina spelt soup". Place dried borlotti beans in a bowl with cold water. Let them soak for a whole night. Spelt should undergo the same process, but for one hour only. Subsequently, cook beans in a pot of boiling salted water together with two cloves of garlic and a few sage leaves. Meanwhile, brown a mirepoix of celery, onion and carrots with olive oil in a very large saucepan. Salt to taste. When beans are ready, drain and keep their broth. Process the beans with a vegetable mill in order to obtain a creamy mixture.

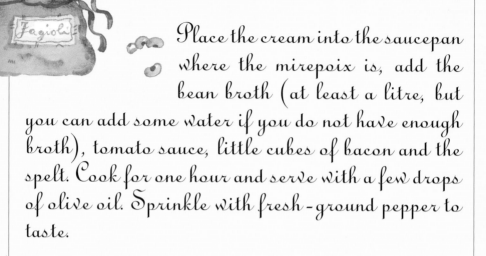

Place the cream into the saucepan where the mirepoix is, add the bean broth (at least a litre, but you can add some water if you do not have enough broth), tomato sauce, little cubes of bacon and the spelt. Cook for one hour and serve with a few drops of olive oil. Sprinkle with fresh-ground pepper to taste.

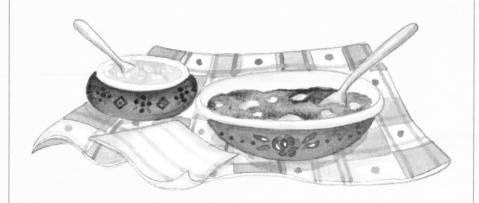

Yellow porridge with Italian black cabbage

1 red onion, tomato sauce, Italian black cabbage, maize flour

This is a typical winter dish, prepared with black cabbage, a type of vegetable almost unknown outside Tuscany. Preparing black cabbage with maize flour was a traditional way of obtaining nutritious and warming food, especially for poor families. You may use quantities of maize flour and black cabbage according to your personal taste: you can decide to make a denser soup adding more flour, or give the soup a stronger cabbage flavour. Clean the black cabbage and remove the hardest parts. Wilt a chopped onion with abundant olive oil in a large pan. Add tomato sauce and black cabbage. Let the mixture simmer until the cabbage nearly dissolves. Add hot water and sprinkle with maize flour gradually. Cook for the time required by the flour you are using: follow the instructions on the package. Serve warm, with a few drops of olive oil.

GARMUGIA IN THE STYLE OF LUCCA

4 small fresh onions, 50 g bacon, 100 g minced beef,
400 g vegetables (peas, artichokes, broad beans, asparagus tips),
broth, olive oil, salt, toasted bread.

Garmugia is an ancient and nutritious soup traditionally prepared by the people of Lucca. It is a typical spring soup, as fresh vegetables are used. Brown chopped onion with olive oil in a large saucepan. Cut the bacon into very thin pieces and place it into the pan. Add the minced and stir using a wooden spoon. Wash and cut vegetables and place them into the pan. Salt to taste. Keep on stirring for 15 minutes. Warm a litre of broth and pour it into the pan. Let the mixture simmer over low heat until all the vegetables are cooked. Place a slice of broiled bread into each soup plate and pour the soup over it. You might as well cut bread into cubes and sprinkle the soup with it.

Carabaccia: a Tuscan onion soup

1 kg red onions, broth, parmigiano cheese,
4 slice homemade bread, olive oil, salt, pepper.

Clean and slice onions. Place them in a casserole - an earthenware casserole would be perfect - add olive oil and brown onions over low heat for about 30 minutes. Stir frequently in order to avoid sticking. Add some salt and a litre of warm broth. Let the soup simmer and reduce for 30 more minutes. Do not cover the pot with the lid. Place a slice of broiled bread into each bowl and pour the soup over the bread. Sprinkle with parmigiano cheese and fresh-ground pepper.
This soup is also called "Florentine onion soup": this version includes chopped carrots and celery. This recipe dates back to the Renaissance and it was originally flavoured with sweet ingredients: sugar, chopped almonds, cinnamon and agresto.

Lombardy soup

1 kg fresh cannellini beans, 4 slices of homemade bread, garlic, sage leaves, olive oil, salt, pepper

This is a very popular dish all over Tuscany, but, despite its name, it is completely unknown in Lombardy! Pour 1.5 litre of salted water in a pot. Add two cloves of garlic, some sage leaves, and some tablespoons of olive oil. Add the beans and cook the mixture. Once ready, remove some beans using a slotted spoon and process them with a vegetable mill. Place the mashed beans into the pot again and stir the soup. Place a slice of broiled bread into each bowl and pour the soup over the bread.
Sprinkle with fresh-ground pepper and a few drops of oil.

Fish soup

1 kg assorted fish, 1 onion, 1 stalk celery, 3 cloves garlic,
3 tomatoes, olive oil, salt

The most suitable types of fish for this soup are tub gunard, scorpion fish, monkfish, weaver fish and john dory fish. Clean the fish carefully and cut it into pieces. Brown chopped celery, carrot, onion and two cloves of garlic with six tablespoons of olive oil in a large saucepan. Add mashed tomatoes and fish. Salt to taste. Let the fish season in this sauce. Remove all the garlic, according to your taste. Pour 1 litre of water into the saucepan and cook for at least 20 minutes. Remove all the pieces of fish with a slotted spoon and process them with a vegetable mill. Add the fish to the sauce and stir gently over low heat for a few minutes.

Caldaro in the style of Argentario

330 g octopus, 200 g cuttlefish, 250g scorpion fish, 250 g weaver fish, 330 g john dory fish, 200g conger eel, 100 g moray eel, 200 g limpets, 400 g tomatoes, 4 slices homemade bread, white wine, 3 cloves garlic, 1 onion, chilli pepper, parsley, olive oil, salt

Caldaro is a traditional soup of the coastal area of Argentario. It looks quite similar to Caciucco, another type of fish soup which is typical of northern Tuscany, especially of Livorno. Scale and clean all the fish and remove entrails. Cut the fish into large pieces. Use head and fishbone of each fish to prepare a broth in a pot with 1 litre of boiling salted water. Once ready, strain the broth using a wire skimmer. Chop onion and parsley and brown them with olive oil in a pan. Add two cloves of garlic and chilli pepper to taste. Roughly cut cuttlefish and octopus and place the pieces into the pan. Salt to taste. Pour white wine onto and tomato sauce onto the fish. If the mixture looks to dry, add some broth. Cook octopus and cuttlefish. Afterwards, add the other types of fish. Cook for 20 minutes more, adding the broth gradually. If you prefer a dense soup, you might as well let it simmer and reduce. Broil 4 slices of bread, rub them with garlic and place them into the soup plates. Pour the soup over the bread and serve it. Red wine is the perfect accompaniment for Caldaro.

Arselle* soup

1,2 kg arselle (banded wedge shells), 2 cloves garlic, parsley, chilli pepper, dry white wine, 400 g ripe tomatoes, 4 slices Tuscan bread, olive oil, salt, pepper

Clean the arselle by soaking them in salted water for at least 12 hours; change the water frequently, in order to eliminate all the sand. Wash arselle under running water. Brown chopped garlic and parsley with six tablespoons of olive oil in a large pan. Add chilli pepper to taste. As soon as garlic changes its colour, pour white wine onto the mixture. Cut tomatoes into cubes and place them into the pan. Salt to taste. Let the sauce simmer and reduce for a few minutes. Subsequently, add arselle and cook for 5 minutes over low heat. Put a lid on the pan until arselle are ready. Broil 4 slices of bread, rub them with garlic and place them into the soup plates. Pour the soup over the bread and serve it.

This recipe can be prepared using clams or razor clams.

*Banded wedge shells should be used for this soup. As it is difficult to find them outside Tuscany, you might as well use other types of clam.

Another type of arselle soup can be made with a slightly different process: let the arselle open by heating them over a brisk flame. When they open, drain them from the broth they have formed. Strain the arselle broth and remove half of the arselle from the shells. Add both the arselle (with and without shell) and the broth to browned chopped garlic.

Main courses

Stuffed chicken neck

2 chicken necks (without feathers and bones), 1 carrot,
1 stalk celery, 1 onion, 100 g minced pork, 250 g minced beef,
50 g butter, thyme, 3 eggs, 50 g grated parmigiano cheese,
50 g breadcrumbs, nutmeg, salt, pepper

Brown minced meat with butter and thyme in a high-sided pan. Prepare a vegetable broth by boiling a carrot, a stalk of celery and an onion in salted water. Place eggs, cheese, breadcrumbs, ground nutmeg, salt, pepper and browned minced meat in a bowl. Stir carefully until all the ingredients combine. Subsequently, stuff the chicken necks with the mixture. Tie both ends of each neck with some kitchen twine and place them into very hot

LAMPREDOTTO IN ZIMINO

600 g lampredotto,
400 g peeled tomatoes,
300 g spinach (or chards), garlic,
chilli pepper, garlic, salt, pepper

Lampredotto is very popular in Florence. It is a common type of tripe sold even on the streets by "Trippai" (tripe sellers), cooked in broth and served with bread and green sauce. Lapredotto is the fourth bovine stomach, also called abomasum. The first three chambers are the rumen (blanket or flat or smooth tripe), the reticulum (honeycomb and pocket tripe), and the omasum (book or bible or leaf tripe). Lampredotto in zimino is an ancient and almost forgotten recipe. Have the butcher clean and blanch the tripe. Cut lampredotto into strips and brown it with little olive oil, chopped garlic and chilli pepper. Let the tripe season and then add tomatoes. Cook for half an hour. Boil roughly chopped spinach in salted water, drain and add them to the tripe. Cook for 15 minutes. Serve warm with fresh-ground pepper.

water. Cook over low heat for half an hour, paying attention not to let water boil. Cool, slice and serve with pickles and vegetables in oil.

Sheep stew

1 kg sheep meat, 1 carrot, 1 onion, 1 stalk celery, 2 cloves garlic, parsley, 400 g peeled tomatoes, red wine, olive oil, broth, vinegar, salt, pepper

Sheep stew is a traditional dish of Campi Bisenzio, a town on the outskirts of Florence, that is why the recipe is also named after this town as "campigiana sheep meat". Nowadays, sheep stew can be found in some restaurants and, more often, at village feasts. Sheep meat is prepared this way in Barberino del Mugello as well, as the two towns are connected by an old route - Provinciale 8, through Passo delle Croci - which has allowed contacts between the two areas for a long time.
Clean the meat carefully; remove all the fat, nerves and

tendons, as they could give the stew a strong bad smell. Soak the meat into water and vinegar for a whole night. Subsequently, cook the meat over low heat briefly, in order to let all its internal water evaporate. In another pan, sauté chopped onion, celery and carrot with olive oil and add sliced meat. Wet the mixture with red wine. Let the wine simmer and reduce and then pour tomatoes on the meat. Sprinkle with salt and pepper to taste. Let the stew cook for at least 2 hours, wetting it with broth if necessary. The stew can be an excellent sauce for penne.

Florentine tripe

1 kg tripe, 500 g ripe tomatoes, 1 carrot, 1 stalk celery, 1 onion, 2 cloves garlic, meat broth, salt, pepper, grated parmigiano cheese

Tripe is a classic in Florentine cooking tradition. In Florence, you can find "trippai" (tripe sellers), who sell tripe and lampredotto on the streets. By the word "tripe", Florentine people mean the three first chambers of bovine stomach: the rumen (blanket or flat or smooth tripe), the reticulum (honeycomb and pocket tripe), and the omasum (book or bible or leaf tripe). The fourth chamber, called abomasums, is also edible and widespread in Florence, where it is also called lampredotto. Have the butcher clean and blanch the tripe. However, wash it again before using it. Cut the tripe into 10-cm-long and 1.5-cm-wide strips and set aside. Sauté chopped onion, carrot and celery with olive oil in a saucepan. When the onion browns, add the tripe and let it season in the mirepoix for a few minutes. Then, add the tomatoes. Wet the tripe with a glass of broth and sprinkle it with salt and pepper to taste. Let the mixture simmer and reduce over low heat for one hour, stirring frequently. Serve very hot with grated parmigiano cheese.

Tripe can be prepared in other ways, according to different Tuscan recipes. Here are a few examples. Tripe in the style of Livorno: replace carrot and celery with abundant garlic and parsley. Tripe in the style of Pisa: add minced beef or pork, chopped ham or bacon to the tripe.

Tripe in the style of Siena: add pork sausages, pecorino cheese and tarragon. Last but not least, tripe in the style of Maremma are made with the recipe of Siena plus minced beef.

RECOOKED BOILED MEAT WITH ONIONS

500 g boiled meat, 800 g onions, 400 g tomato sauce,
2 cloves garlic, sage leaves, olive oil, salt, pepper

Brown whole cloves of garlic with olive oil in a pan. Add some sage leaves and thinly chopped onions. When onions look golden, pour tomato sauce on them and sprinkle with salt and pepper to taste. Let ingredients combine for a few minutes and then place sliced boiled meat into the sauce. Let tomato sauce reduce over low heat until the sauce is dense. Another recipe for this dish suggests to add chopped celery and thinly sliced bacon, plus dried mushrooms at the end of cooking time. Dried mushrooms should be hydrated in lukewarm water before usage. Using boiled meat of the previous day is a tasty way of avoiding any waste of food.

Florentine marrowbones

4 beef marrowbones, 1 onion, garlic, Marsala or Vin Santo, flour, thyme, 500 g tomato flesh, broth, salt, pepper

Skin and flour marrowbones. Sauté roughly chopped onion and garlic with olive oil in a pan which should be large enough to contain four marrowbones. Add some thyme and place the marrowbones into the pan. Brown them on both sides and wet with Marsala or Vin Santo. Let the wine reduce over brisk flame. Turn the meat frequently on both sides. Subsequently, add tomato, a glass of broth, salt and pepper. Allow cooking over low heat until the sauce is very dense and the meat softens. Members of my family add lemon peel before serving the dish. Lemon should be organic. You might as well prepare this dish without tomato.

Peposo in the style of Impruneta

(pepper beef stew)

800 g beef muscle, 200 g peeled tomatoes, garlic, red wine, salt, ground black pepper, black pepper grains

This is a traditional dish of Impruneta, a village in the Fiorentine hills, which is very famous for its earthenware pottery. Craftsmen used to cook the stew on the edge of kilns, letting it simmer slowly for a very long time. A legend tells this stew was invented by those craftsmen who manufactured bricks for Brunelleschi's dome of Santa Maria del Fiore. Certainly, this recipe was not possible before the Fifteenth century, as pepper was a very expensive spice at that time. Another name for this dish is "Peposo alla Fornacina", wich means "Peposo cooked in the kiln by the craftsmen". Muscle is not a valuable meat cut: it has fat and that allows cooking without any oil or fat.

Cut the muscle into rough pieces and place it in a large pan. Add some cloves of garlic, a glass of red wine (possibly Chianti; use the same wine that accompanies the dish), tomato and salt. Sprinkle with a tablespoon of fresh-ground pepper. If you decide to obtain a more garnished dish, add both ground pepper and pepper grains. Cover the meat with hot water and cook for at least 2 hours, stirring occasionally. Add more water if necessary. At the and of cooking time, meat should be very soft and its sauce well reduced. Serve with Chianti and slices of Tuscan bread.

Today, Peposo is prepared in a pan, but if you own a wood stove, use it to cook this stew. In this case, an earthenware pan would be appropriate.

RED MULLETS IN THE STYLE OF LIVORNO

12 red mullets (they should be 100g each), 500 g peeled tomatoes, 2 cloves garlic, parsley, olive oil, salt

Heat abundant olive oil in a pan large enough to contain all the red mullets. Chop the cloves of garlic and parsley. Brown half the chopped ingredients with olive oil. Subsequently, add tomatoes and salt to taste. If you wish, sprinkle with some chilli pepper. Let the sauce reduce a little and then place the fish in the pan. Cook over low heat for 10 minutes. Turn red mullets on both sides only if you are sure not to break them. Occasionally, shake the pan very gently.

Sprinkle with the remaining chopped garlic and parsley. This dish is very simple and gives an excellent result when the fish is very fresh.

Florentine steak

1 T - bone steaks (chianina beef or maremmana beef), salt, pepper

The T-bone should weigh around 700g and be 2 or 3 cm thick. Prepare one of it for each person. This is a well-known recipe all over the world. What we call "steak" in Tuscany corresponds to a T-bone in the rest of Italy. We also call it simply "fiorentina" (Florentine). This meat cut comes from chianina or maremmana cow short loin or tenderloin and it must be prepared with its bone. It is served very rare but it should never be raw or cold inside. Never practice holes with a fork on it while cooking. The best way of cooking this type of meat is broiling it over wood fire. Remove the T-bone steak from the fridge at least 2 hours before cooking it. Prepare the fire and then place it on a very hot grill for 4 or 5 minutes. Turn it on the other side using a cooking spatula or your own hands and broil for the same time. Sprinkle both sides with salt and place the steak on a tray. You might as well use a grate on a gas burner. Serve hot, as it becomes tough when it cools. Wet it with olive oil and sprinkle with fresh-ground pepper. The best side dish for t-bone steak is faglioli all' uccelletto or salad.

Chine of pork

1 kg loin (with its bone), garlic, rosemary, olive oil, salt, pepper

Mix chopped garlic (two cloves), rosemary, salt and pepper in a bowl. Place one third of this mixture between the meat and its bone, one third on the chine of pork and one third on the external meat. Tie the meat with kitchen twine and place it in a casserole, sprinkle with olive oil and bake at medium heat for about one hour. Turn it on both sides and wet it with its cooking juice. Once ready, remove the kitchen twine, slice it and place it on tray. Wet it with some cooking juice. Serve warm or cold, as it is tasty in both ways. Artusi describes this recipe as " roast chine of pork, served cold as, in this way, it tastes much better than hot. Chine of pork is a loin with ribs, that can weighs 3 or

4 kilograms" According to a legend, the recipe dates back to 1430, when a council between the catholic church and the orthodox church was held in Florence. This dish was served to the participants and the Greek bishops show their appreciation by saying the word "aristos" (excellent). That is why this meat cut is called arista in Italian language.

Arrosto morto (pot roast)

800 g beef topside, 1 onion, 1 carrot, 1 stalk celery, red wine, bay leaves, broth, olive oil, salt, pepper

Tie the meat with kitchen twine. Chop onion, carrot, and celery and sauté them with abundant olive oil and some bay leaves. Once wilted, add the meat and brown it on both sides. Wet it with a glass of wine and sprinkle with salt and pepper to taste. As the alcohol evaporates, add two glasses of broth. Let the juice reduce for 90 minutes. Once ready, remove the kitchen twine and serve the hot slices of meat covered with the remaining cooking juice. This recipe is widespread all over Tuscany and its directions are also suitable for other types of meat, such as rabbit meat. It is advisable to cover the toughest and driest parts with lard. If you prepare rabbit meat, use white wine. You might as well reduce the basic aromatic ingredients to garlic and rosemary only.

WILD BOAR IN THE STYLE OF MAREMMA

800 g young wild boar meat, 500 g ripe tomatoes or peeled tomatoes, 1 carrot, 1 onion, 1 stalk celery, garlic, bay leaves, red wine, vinegar, olive oil, salt, pepper

Clean the meat carefully and cut it into pieces. Slice carrot, celery and onion. Prepare a marinade with half a litre of red wine, half a glass of vinegar, sliced ingredients, two cloves of garlic and some bay leaves. Soak the meat into the sauce and marinate for 12 hours. Remove the vegetables from the sauce with a slotted spoon and sauté them with half a glass of olive oil in a large pan. As they wilt, add the meat and cook for a few minutes over brisk flame. Pour some marinade on it and let the alcohol evaporate. Finally, add tomatoes and sprinkle with salt and pepper. Cook from 2 to 3 hours. Wet with water or broth if necessary. Serve the meat with the cooking juice. You might strain the juice, if you wish.

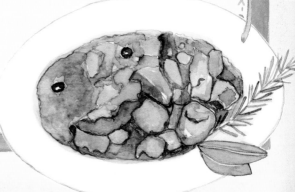

Roast wild boar

800 g young wild boar meat, 50 g bacon, garlic, red wine, broth, olive oil, salt, pepper

Young wild boar does not need to be marinated and it is prepared like pork. If the wild boar is not young, it could become tough when it roasts, so make sure the meat really comes from a young animal before cooking it. The thigh is the most suitable part of a wild boar for this recipe. Slice some bacon into strips and season with salt, pepper and garlic. Wrap the wild boar meat with all the bacon strips and place it in a casserole with abundant olive oil. Sprinkle with salt and pepper to taste. Bake in oven for a few minutes, turning the meat on both sides. Pour two glasses of broth on the meat and bake for one hour. Serve with agresto, mustard or apple sauce.

Spicy wild boar meat

1 kg wild boar meat (possibly of a young wild boar),
1 stalk celery, 1 onion, 1 carrot, rosemary, garlic, olive oil, sage
leaves, bay leaves, cloves, juniper berries, a sachet saffron,
red wine, olive oil, salt, pepper

Clean the meat carefully and cut it into pieces, eliminating fat parts and nerves. Roughly chop carrot, celery and onion and mix them with half a litre of red wine and all the spices except saffron. Soak the meat into the sauce and season for 12 hours. Remove all the chopped ingredients with a slotted spoon, thinly chop them and brown them in a large pan with half a glass of olive oil. As the ingredients wilt, add the meat. Cook it a few minutes over brisk flame and then wet it with the marinade. Sprinkle with salt and pepper. Cook over low heat from 2 to 3 hours, adding water or broth if necessary. Before removing the pan from heat, add saffron diluted in some water.

Hare with dolceforte sauce

1,5 kg hare meat (possibly well hung hare meat), 60 g bacon or fat
dry-cured ham, 2 carrots, 2 onions, 2 stalks celery, garlic,
rosemary, bay leaves, sage leaves, red wine, vinegar, 50 g candied
citron or candied orange, cloves, 50 g pine nuts, 50g raisin, 50 g
grated dark chocolate, sugar, broth, olive oil, salt, pepper

This dish dates back to the Renaissance, when
seasoning meat with sweet ingredients, vinegar and
agresto was a widespread habit due to the need of
hiding the bad smell and the bad preservation of the
meat itself. Moreover, this was a nobles' dish, as
poor people could not afford the cost of these refined
ingredients. It became much more popular in the
Nineteenth century as a bourgeois dish. Clean the
meat and run it under water. Cut it into pieces and
place them in a bowl with chopped celery, carrot and
onion. Cover with red wine and vinegar and marinate
for 12 hours. Once ready, remove the meat from the

marinade and wash it again. Set aside a glass of dip for cooking the meat later. Place the meat in a pot covered with a lid and let it eliminate all its internal water. Chop carrot, onion, celery, garlic, rosemary and bacon. Place the chopped ingredients in a pan with olive oil and start cooking. Add sage and bay leaves. When they wilt, add the hare meat, salt and pepper. As the meat browns, pour a glass of red wine on it and let all the alcohol evaporate. Cook wetting with broth when necessary. At the end of cooking time, the dip should be abundant.

While the meat cooks, prepare the dolceforte sauce. Mix half a glass of broth, half a glass of vinegar, candied fruits, two chopped cloves, pine nuts, raisin, grated chocolate and sugar. Stir well. A few minutes before the hare meat is ready, pour dolceforte sauce into the pot and cook it. Allow cooling before serving the dish. Some people suggest that this dish should be eaten the day after its preparation. The same recipe can be used for wild boar meat.

Etruscan-style rabbit

1 rabbit (about 1 Kg), 250 g black olives, 90 g bacon, 1 carrot, 1 onion, 1 stalk celery, sage leaves, rosemary, garlic, white wine, broth, olive oil, salt, pepper

Eliminate head and legs. Remove the liver and set aside. Cut the meat into pieces. Chop a carrot, an onion, a stalk of celery, two cloves of garlic and brown the mirepoix with bacon cubes and olive oil in a large pan. Add the meat and brown it briefly over brisk flame. Improve the flavour with some sage leaves, rosemary and a glass of white wine. Let the alcohol evaporate and then sprinkle with salt and pepper to taste. Before the end of cooking time, add chopped liver. Once the meat is ready, remove it from the pan and process the sauce with a vegetable mill. Afterwards, cook strained sauce and meat together for 15 more minutes. Add black olives when the cooking time has almost passed.

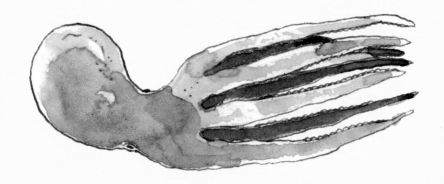

Drunken octopus

1 kg octopus, 1 celery, 1 carrot, 1 onion, 3 cloves garlic, bay leaves,
½ l red wine, parsley, olive oil, salt

This dish is usually served as a main course in Livorno, but it can also be served as an appetizer on a bruschetta, or as a side dish together with salad, or even used as a sauce for spaghetti. Clean the octopus, removing its entrails. Wash and soften by using a meat pounder. Octopus can also be frozen in order to be softened. Cut it into large pieces, as its meat reduce while cooking. Sauté chopped onion, carrot, celery, cloves of garlic and bay leaves with olive oil in a pan, possibly an earthenware pan. Add octopus peaces and brown it for a few minutes with its cooking water. Pour almost all the wine and cook for 40 minutes, until the octopus becomes soft. Taste and add salt if necessary. If the sauce reduces too much, add some water. When the fish is almost ready, pour the remaining wine and sprinkle with freshly chopped parsley. Cool and serve covered with abundant dip.

If you decide to serve it as an appetizer, toast some bread, place a slice on each bowl, and pour the sauce over the bread. In this case, octopus should be cut into very small pieces.

STUFFED CELERY
IN THE STYLE OF PRATO

4 celeries, 2 eggs, 50 g flour, 400 g meat sauce,
Stuffing: 300 g beef, 150 chicken livers, 150 chicken breast,
50 g parmigiano cheese, 2 eggs, olive oil, salt, pepper

Stuffed celery is an autumn dish usually prepared in the area around Prato. Several versions of this ancient recipe are possible, according to the ingredients available or to the need of consuming leftovers. First of all, prepare the stuffing. Cook beef meat, chicken livers and chicken breast with olive oil. If you wish, add some chopped onion. Once ready, grind all the meat and mix it with two eggs, grated parmigiano cheese and salt and pepper to taste. Chop the best stalks of celery and cut them lengthwise. Blanch celery in boiling salted water, cool and cut the stalks into 10-cm-long pieces. Place the stuffing on each stalk, make two stalks stick with the stuffing in the middle and tie with kitchen twine. Go on like this with all the stalks. Rub the stuffed celery with some flour and fry them in boiling oil. Heat some meat sauce in a pan and put fried celery into the sauce. Let the sauce reduce a little while the celery gains flavour over low heat. Remove the twine before serving. Chicken livers and chicken breast could be replaced with mortadella*. If you wish, add grated nutmeg to the stuffing and cook the meat in a mirepoix of carrot, celery and onion.

*Mortadella is a type of salted pork

Florentine salt cod

800 g hydrated salt cod, flour, 500 g ripe tomatoes, 1 onion, garlic, sage leaves, parsley, olive oil, salt, pepper

This recipe is also called "salt cod in the style of Livorno". Salt cod is devoid of head, cut lengthwise and preserved with salt. Remove skin and fishbone from the fish. Cut it into 8-cm-wide cubes and rub the cubes with flour. Heat olive oil in a pan, add sage leaves, a whole clove of garlic and fry the fish cubes. Remove the fish using a slotted spoon and place them on kitchen paper. Slice an onion and let it wilt in another pan with two cloves of garlic and olive oil. At this point, add pieces of tomato, salt and pepper. Cook for 20 minutes and then add the fish cubes, allowing cooking for 10 more minutes. Sprinkle with chopped parsley and serve warm.

Salt cod in zimino

600 g hydrated salt cod, 500 g ripe tomatoes, 600 g chards,
1 onion, garlic, olive oil, salt, pepper

The word "zimino" refers to the way of preparing fish (salt cod, cuttlefish, eel and squills) with chards or spinach. It is a Tuscan word, but its origin is unknown. Thinly chop onion, two cloves of garlic, and let them wilt with olive oil in a pan. Slice salt cod and place it into the pan. Brown the fish on both sides for 5 minutes, sprinkle with salt and pepper and let reduce for 20 minutes. Meanwhile, boil chards, drain, squeeze gently to remove all the water, eliminate the white stalks and cut chards into pieces. Add the chards to the tomatoes and place the salt cod in the sauce. Cook for 15 minutes.

There might be different ways of preparing salt cod. It is possible to sauté salt cod in a mirepoix of chopped onion, celery and carrot. You might as well cook chards with tomatoes, allowing a longer cooking time of at least half an hour.

Mantis shrimp stew

2 kg mantis shrimps, 500 g ripe tomatoes, garlic, parsley,
chilli pepper, white wine, Tuscan bread, olive oil, salt

Mantis shrimp is a type of crustacean endowed with many names, like for example "pannocchia" or "canocchia". Clean the mantis shrimps and remove the thorns on their sides. Chop parsley, chilli pepper and three cloves of garlic. Sauté all the chopped ingredients with olive oil. When the garlic browns, add the mantis shrimps and let the fish gain flavour. Pour some white wine and let it evaporate. Add tomatoes, salt and pepper and cook for about 20 minutes. Toast the bread and place a slice of bread in each soup plate. Pour the mantis shrimp stew over the bread. Sprinkle with chopped parsley and serve hot.

BEANS IN A FIASCO

400 g dried canellini beans,
2 cloves garlic, sage leaves, olive oil, salt, pepper

Here is a classic ancient Tuscan recipe, that tells how to prepare a good winter dish, dressed with "olio novo" (fresh-milled oil). The original recipe requires some specific "tools": an old Tuscan fiasco, devoid of its straw, a fireplace and ashes that allow a slow cooking. Tuscan cookware shops sell conic bottles that can replace the fiasco: these bottles can be used to cook beans on a common burner. The night before cooking the beans, soak them in water. Then insert the beans in the fiasco with five tablespoons of olive oil, whole cloves of garlic, some sage leaves, salt and pepper. Cover the mixture with water, reaching two thirds of the fiasco. More water could spill out from the fiasco while cooking. If you use a Tuscan fiasco, close it with yellow paper, cotton wool and oakum so as to let steam go out. Place the fiasco among the ashes of the fireplace, making it stand upright or hang it on a hook above the ashes. Cook for 2 hours until water reduces. Serve in a bowl with olive oil and fresh-ground pepper.

Scorpion fish in the style of Livorno

1.5 kg scorpion fish, 500 g ripe tomatoes, garlic, parsley, broth, olive oil, salt, pepper

Clean the fish carefully. Remove thorns, entrails, gills, fins and scales. Heat abundant olive oil in a saucepan. Place pieces of tomato, two cloves of garlic and parsley into the pan. Cook for a few minutes. Lay the fish in a casserole and pour the sauce on it. Sprinkle with salt and pepper to taste. Pre-heat oven and bake the fish for 45 minutes. Wet with some broth if necessary.

Stockfish with chards

600 g hydrated stockfish (or 375 g dried stockfish),
300 g ripe toamtoes, 1kg chards, 1 carrot, 1 onion, 1 stalk celery,
garlic, parsley, cloves, olive oil, salt, pepper

Stockfish is dried cod. Drying is an ancient way of preserving food, even older than salt-preserved food. Salt-preserved cod is called "baccalà", while dried cod is called "stoccafisso". This is a traditional dish of Versilia, the northern part of the Tuscan coast. It is usually served with some polenta.[*] Remove fishbone and skin from the stockfish. Cut the fish into pieces and set aside. Wash chards, eliminate the white stem and chop them roughly. Thinly chop carrot, onion, a stalk of celery, garlic and parsley. Sauté this mirepoix with abundant olive oil and two cloves. Let the vegetables wilt and add the tomatoes, chards and the pieces of stockfish. Cook over medium heat for one hour, stirring frequently.

[*]Cornflour porridge

CUTTLEFISH IN ZIMINO

800 g clean cuttlefish, 400 g ripe tomatoes, 800 g chards (or spinach), parsley, garlic, white wine, olive oil, salt, pepper

Cut the cuttlefish into strips, wash and dry. Wash and boil chards, drain and remove the white stem in the middle. Roughly chop the chards. Then sauté abundant chopped parsley and three cloves of garlic. Add the cuttlefish and, after a few minutes, wet them with white wine. Let the wine evaporate, add pieces of tomatoes, salt and pepper to taste. Cook for 30 minutes. At this point, place the chards into the pan and cook for 5 more minutes. Serve lukewarm. A variation on this recipe includes a mirepoix of chopped onion, carrot and celery among the ingredients to be browned. You might as well add raw chards to the cuttlefish, cooking for 15 minutes.
Tomatoes can be replaced with the natural black ink of the cuttlefish.

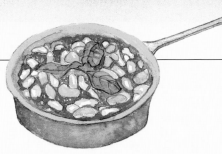

Fagioli all' ucccelletto (beans in a jar)

1 kg fresh canellini beans or 400 g dried canellini beans,
400 g tomato sauce, garlic, sage leaves, olive oil, salt, pepper

This is a traditional Florentine side dish, but it can be found in the area of Mugello as well. It is advisable to use fresh beans, if possible. The origin of this picturesque name has never been explained, although several hypothesis have been proposed. Shell beans and cook them in 2 litres of salted water in a large pot. Cook slowly over low heat. Water may simmer but never really boil or beans might break. Cool and drain. Heat olive oil in a large pan - an earthenware pan would be perfect - and sauté four chopped cloves of garlic and some sage leaves. When garlic browns, add warm beans, sprinkle with salt and pepper and stir gently with a wooden spoon. Pour tomato sauce on the beans and add some sage leaves. Let the mixture reduce until it is rather dense. Pay attention to keep the beans whole. Fagioli all'uccelletto can properly accompany Florentine tripe. Personally, I cook a sausage together with beans, so as to transform a side dish into a main course.

Peas in the Florentine style

500 g shelled fresh peas, 50g bacon or Tuscan rigatino, garlic, sugar, parsley, oil, salt, pepper

This is a spring dish, usually prepared in Florence at the end of April when it is easier to find fresh peas, garlic and parsley. Sauté chopped bacon and whole cloves of garlic with olive oil. Out of season, two or three cloves are enough. When garlic browns, add peas and cover with water. Then, sprinkle with parsley leaves, salt and pepper. If peas are fresh, a short cooking time is enough. However, it is advisable to let water reduce. Before turning off the burner, add a tablespoon of sugar and stir.

Fried pumpkin flowers

16 pumpkin flowers, flour, 1 egg, beer, olive oil, salt, pepper, frying oil.

Make a batter by mixing 100g flour, an egg yolk, two tablespoon olive oil, salt and a glass of beer. Stir until all the ingredients combine. You might as well prepare the batter with water, flour and salt. Clean the flowers, trim off the stem, remove the pistil and wash them. Soak the flowers in the batter and deep fry them in boiling water. Dry the flowers with kitchen paper and serve hot. Whole flowers can be used to make a delicious omelette as well.

Sauces and dips

Meat sauce

400 g beef (sliced or cut into small pieces), 300g tomatoes,
1 onion, 1 carrot, 1 stalk celery, olive oil, red wine, salt, pepper

Chop carrot, celery and onion and sauté the mixture with olive oil in a saucepan. Add the meat and brown it. Pour a glass of red wine onto the meat. Add tomatoes, salt and pepper to taste. Let the sauce cook for half an hour. This Tuscan meat sauce is quite different from the common Italian meat ragout. The recipe of meat ragout includes minced meat, milk, broth or water and meat must cook in tomato sauce.

Fake ragout

(meatless sauce)

500 g tomatoes, 1 onion, 1 stalk celery, 1 carrot,
parsley, red wine, olive oil, salt, pepper

This sauce has ancient origins. Tuscan people call it "fake" since it looks as if it is made of meat, but in fact it does not contain any. Chop the carrot, celery, onion and parsley roughly. Place the mirepoix into a large saucepan, add olive oil and brown it. Pour red wine into the saucepan and let the alcohol evaporate. Add tomatoes. Both peeled tomatoes and fresh ripe tomatoes can be used. Season with salt and pepper to taste. Allow the sauce to simmer over low heat for 30 minutes until reduced. Stir frequently. The sauce is ready when it looks very dense.

Anchovy dip

4 anchovies, 1 clove garlic, olive oil

This traditional dip is used to accompany boiled Tuscan white beans or to season different types of pasta. It is still served with the T-bone steak in some Tuscan restaurants. Clean the anchovies and remove the fishbone. Wash them rapidly. Pour 4 tablespoons of olive oil in a saucepan and brown some roughly chopped garlic. Add the fillets and let them dissolve using a wooden spoon. Remove all the garlic and stir.

An even tastier dip has chopped capers inside. Add capers immediately after removing garlic from the pan.

AGRESTO SAUCE

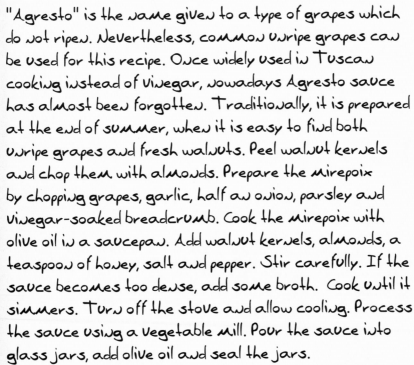

*200 g unripe grapes, 5 walnut kernels,
10 peeled almond, breadcrumb, garlic, onion, parsley,
honey, red vinegar, salt, pepper*

"Agresto" is the name given to a type of grapes which do not ripen. Nevertheless, common unripe grapes can be used for this recipe. Once widely used in Tuscan cooking instead of vinegar, nowadays Agresto sauce has almost been forgotten. Traditionally, it is prepared at the end of summer, when it is easy to find both unripe grapes and fresh walnuts. Peel walnut kernels and chop them with almonds. Prepare the mirepoix by chopping grapes, garlic, half an onion, parsley and vinegar-soaked breadcrumb. Cook the mirepoix with olive oil in a saucepan. Add walnut kernels, almonds, a teaspoon of honey, salt and pepper. Stir carefully. If the sauce becomes too dense, add some broth. Cook until it simmers. Turn off the stove and allow cooling. Process the sauce using a vegetable mill. Pour the sauce into glass jars, add olive oil and seal the jars.

The sauce gains a stronger taste if chopped capers and a salted anchovy are included in it. It usually accompanies both roasted and boiled meat.

Desserts

Anancini

300 g flour, 1 glass olive oil, salt, yeast, anise seeds

An anancino is a salted ring-shaped or double-bubble-shaped biscuit, made in the bakeries of Siena and Grosseto all year round. It is also called "stinco di morto" (a dead man's shinbone) or "biscotto lesso" (boiled biscuit), as they should be soft and dry inside and crisp on the outside. Mix flour with oil, water and yeast. Add salt and anise seeds gradually and knead. When the dough is smooth, give the biscuits the shape you prefer, be it a ring or a double-bubble. Let them rise for 10 minutes. Cook the biscuits briefly in a pot of boiling water, until they float on the surface. Remove them from the pot with a slotted spoon, dry them with some kitchen paper and bake at 180°C for half an hour.

These biscuits used to replace bread in the peasants' diet as they could be stored for a long time.

Berlingozzo

400 g flour, 2 eggs, 2 yolks, 200 g sugar, 100 g butter, 1 lemon (possibly organic), 1 sachet baking powder, salt

Berlingozzo is a traditional Carnival cake, whose ancient origins are linked with the area of Prato and Pistoia. It dates back to the Age of the Medici and its name is probably derived from the word "Berlingaccio", that is "Last Thursday before Lent". Whisk eggs with sugar and then add melted butter. Subsequently, add flour, a pinch of salt, grated lemon peel and baking powder in the end. Stir until the batter is soft and smooth. If it looks too dry, pour a little milk onto it. Spoon the mixture into a greased and floured mould.
Bake at 150°C for 40 minutes.
Berlingozzo of Lamporecchio, another type of Berlingozzo, is made with anise seeds and devoid of yeast. It looks quite similar to Brigidini pastries.

FLORENTINE CARNIVAL CAKE

2 eggs, 2 ½ tablespoons sugar,
2 oranges (possibly organic),
400 g flour, 10 tablespoons olive oil,
1 cup milk, 1 teaspoon baking powder,
salt, icing sugar, cocoa powder

This is a traditional Florentine Carnival cake.
This is my family recipe, handed over without any precise measures but cups and spoons. Whisk two eggs in a bowl. Add sugar and stir vigorously so that it combines with the eggs. Grate orange peel and add it to the mixture. Sprinkle with flour gradually and stir. Subsequently, add olive oil and lukewarm milk. When all the ingredients combine, add the baking powder. Pour the mixture into a greased casserole and place it into the oven at 200°C. Bake for 35 minutes. When the top of the cake looks golden, remove from oven and allow cooling. Sprinkle with icing sugar. Draw a Florentine lily on a sheet of paper, cut it out and place it over the cake and sprinkle with cocoa powder. Either unsweetened or sweet cocoa powder can be used. The cake can be also garnished with cream or chantilly cream.

Brigidini of Lamporecchio

3 eggs, 180 g sugar, 1 pinch salt, anisette (or 1 tablespoon anise seeds), flour, a Brigidini mould or a waffle iron.

Brigidino is a small round thin crisp waffle. Whisk eggs in a bowl with a tablespoon of anisette (or crushed anise seeds). Stir the batter adding enough flour to make it rather firm. Form small balls using a teaspoon or your hands. Place the balls of dough into the hot waffle iron, turning it to both sides. Brigidino is a typical confectionery product of Lamporecchio, near Pistoia, and according to tradition it was born by mistake in the convent bakery of Bridgettine sisters, who used to bake hosts.

Pellegrino Artusi, a famous Italian gourmet and culinary critic, described Brigidini as ``a dessert

QUARESIMALI
(Lenten Almond Biscuits)

*200 g flour, 200 g sugar, 50 g unsweetened cocoa powder,
1 sachet vanilla, 1 teaspoon baking powder, 3 egg whites*

Quaresimali are very simple alphabet-letter-shaped biscuits, which used to be prepared for little children in Florence during Lent. Their dough is devoid of egg yolks, as this food was forbidden during Lent. The dark golden colour of these biscuits, due to cocoa powder, was once obtained using caramelised sugar.

Sift flour with sugar and cocoa powder. Once sifted, add vanilla and baking powder to the mixture. Whisk egg whites in a bowl until stiff. Add the stiff egg whites to the sifted mixture and stir gently in order to obtain a dense creamy batter. If you think it is necessary to make the batter creamier, add another stiff egg white. Place the mixture into an icing bag and draw letters of the alphabet over a baking tray covered with a baking sheet. There should be enough room between the letters, since the batter leavens while cooking. Let it stand for a while and then bake at 150°C for 15 minutes. These biscuits were difficult to find in a recent past, since their production had almost disappeared. Nowadays, Quaresimali are easy to find in supermarkets and bakeries. Another version of this recipe includes grated orange peel or hazelnut paste.

and a delight of Tuscany, where they are served on every occasion, even at fairs and village feasts, during which they are cooked in public on a hot waffle iron." They used to be cooked on a waffle iron called "giostra" (carrousel) directly at the stalls.

Ugly but good meringues

300 g peeled sweet almonds, 10 g peeled bitter almonds, 250 g sugar, 3 egg white, 1 wafer sheet

Nutty meringues have a rough and ugly appearance. Nevertheless, they taste particularly good. Their recipe is widespread in the area around Prato and they used to be sold exclusively with "Prato Biscuits" in the past.

Toast almonds for a few minutes in the oven and chop them very thinly. Add almonds to the sugar and stir. In another bowl, whisk egg whites until stiff. Subsequently, add sugar and almonds gradually. The batter should become rather firm.

Spoon the batter on a wafer sheet or on a greased and floured baking tray, forming small balls. Bake at 150°C for 30 minutes, until meringues become golden and their surface starts to crack. This dessert could be accompanied by Vin Santo.

Rice fritters

1 kg original rice, 2 l milk, 600 g sugar, 4 oranges (possibly organic), salt, 10 eggs, 650 g raisin, half glass Marsala (or Cognac), 50 g flour, oil for frying

Rice fritters, or Saint Joseph's fritters, are prepared all over Tuscany on 19th March, Saint Joseph's Day. Nowadays, these fritters can be found in bakeries and bars for a couple of weeks during the month of March. The members of my family prepare these fritters on the first Sunday after Saint Joseph's Day and give them, on small trays, to friends and relatives. This is my family recipe and shows suitable quantities for the family needs. The night before making these fritters, prepare a mixture with rice, cold milk, sugar, grated orange peel and a pinch of salt. Cook over low heat until boiling. When it boils, allow cooking for the time usually required by the type of rice you are preparing. Avoid sticking by using the wire gauze over the flame. The following day, place raisin in lukewarm water in order to hydrate it. When it is ready, dry it and rub it with flour. Sift it to eliminate any exceeding flour. Add salt to taste, eggs, raisin and Marsala. Stir to make all the ingredients combine. Heat oil in frying pan. Prepare small balls of batter using a spoon and deep fry them in boiling oil. Remove the small balls when they start floating on the surface of the oil. Dry fritters with kitchen.

Scarpaccia Viareggina
(zucchini tart in the style of Viareggio)

2 eggs, 1 cup sugar, 100 g butter, flour, milk,
5 zucchinis, raisin, salt

This tart is both sweet and salted. It used to be a main course, but today it is served as a dessert. This is my family recipe. Place eggs, a cup of sugar and a pinch of salt in a large bowl. Stir well and then add melted butter, a glass of flour and a glass of milk. The mixture should be rather liquid. Wash and thinly slice zucchinis. Add them to the batter together with some raisin. Grease a casserole, pour the mixture and bake at low heat for one hour.

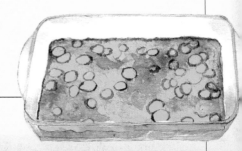

BUCCELLATO

400 g flour, 125 g sugar, 40 g butter, 20 g yeast, 2 eggs,
1 glass milk, 50 g raisin, 10 anise seeds, salt

This is a traditional ring-shaped cake of Lucca and it is sold
daily in bakeries. A proverb tells that 'Chi viene a Lucca e 'un
mangia il buccellato è come se 'un ci fosse stato' (if you have
come to Lucca and you have not tasted Buccellato, it is like
not having been there at all).
Mix flour with sugar and a pinch of salt on a pastry board. In
a well in the middle of the flour pour eggs and add butter, milk
and yeast. Yeast must be reactivated in lukewarm water,
whilst butter should be slightly melted. Set aside a little of
egg white to brush the cake. Knead the dough until it is firm,
soft and smooth. If it becomes to dry and difficult to knead,
wet it with water. When it is ready, add raisin and crushed
anise seeds. Give the dough a ring shape. Place the cake in a
lukewarm room, cover it with a kitchen towel and let it rise for
at least one hour. Pre-heat oven at 150°C.
Brush the top of the cake with egg
white and bake for 45 minutes.
This dessert can be served
together with wine,
especially Vin Santo.
As it gets stale and dry,
Buccellato can be dipped
into milk at breakfas

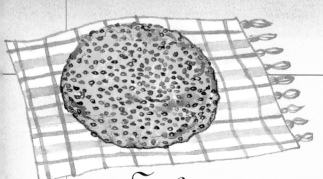

Schiacciata con l' uva
(Wine Grape Cake)

350 g flour, 20 g yeast, water, 800 g black grapes, 150 g sugar, olive oil, salt (flour, water and yeast might be replaced with leavened bread dough).

This is a traditional cake prepared in Florence and in the area of Chianti in autumn, during the grape harvest. It is easy to find in Tuscan bakeries. If you decide to prepare the bread dough yourself, start preparing it three hours before serving the cake. Obviously, you can use bread dough bought at the baker's. Place flour, yeast and a glass of water on a pastry board and knead. Cover the dough ball with a kitchen towel and let it stand at room temperature for at least one hour. Once ready, knead the dough again with olive oil. When the olive oil is completely absorbed, add sugar and a pinch of salt. Go on kneading. Subsequently, take half of the dough and roll it out and place it into a mould, covering half the depth of its sides. Detach each grape from the bunches. Wash the grapes and place them on the rolled out dough in the mould. Sprinkle with sugar and a few drops of oil. Roll out the remaining dough and place it over the grapes. Fold its edges to make them stick to the first dough sheet. Arrange the remaining grapes and sugar on the second sheet. Wet the surface of the cake with little olive oil and bake at 200°C for 30 minutes, until the upper layer of the sheet becomes golden. Serve when lukewarm or cold. It is possible to make little changes to this recipe: for example, try adding lukewarm olive oil, seasoned with rosemary, to the bread dough.

Castagnaccio

(chestnut flour cake)

250 g chestnut flour, 100 g raisin, 80 g pine nuts,
rosemary, water, salt, olive oil

Chestnut flour cakes are very popular in the Appenini mountains and even though there are only slight differences in the recipe of each area, this dessert has several names: migliaccio dolce, baldino (in Arezzo), toppone (in Siena). It is an autumn recipe, as in that season the fresher chestnut flour can be easily found. Soak the raisin in a bowl of lukewarm water for 15 minutes. Sift all the chestnut flour and place it into a tall mixing-bowl and add lukewarm water stirring gently. The batter should become rather liquid and without any lumps. Add a tablespoon of olive oil, a pinch of salt, drained raisin and two thirds of pine nuts. Place the mixture into a greased mould. Once in the mould, the height of the mixture should not exceed 1 cm. Garnish the surface with rosemary-needles and pine nuts. Pre-heat oven at 180°C and bake for 35 minutes. Serve when lukewarm or cold accompanied by new wine.

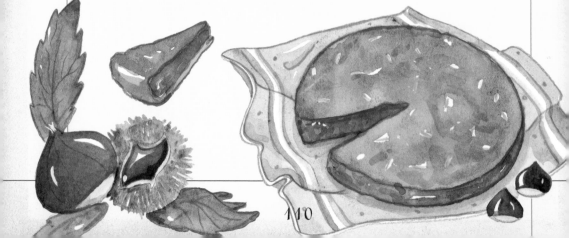

This is the way castagnaccio is prepared by the members of my family, but higher or crisper castagnaccio types can be found around Tuscany. There are richer chestnut flour cakes which are 2cm high, especially in the area of Livorno. Pine nuts can be replaced with walnuts. Moreover, the basic batter of flour, water and olive oil can be gradually spooned in boiling oil, so as to obtain small delicious fritters.

Cenci (Carnival fritters)

240 g flour, 2 eggs, 40 g sugar, 20 g butter, liquor
(rum, maraschino cherry liquor, brandy, marsala),
vanilla sugar, oil for frying, salt

Cenci are a traditional fried dessert made all over Tuscany at Carnival. Prepare a dough with flour, eggs, sugar, melted butter, a pinch of salt and a shot glass of liquor. Knead and once ready, rub the ball of dough with flour, cover it with a kitchen towel and let it stand for half an hour. This dough should result rather firm, if not, add more flour. Roll out the dough until it is ½ cm high and cut it into 10-centimetre-long and 5-centimetre-wide strips by using a pastry wheel. Decide the right shape for your Cenci: you can have strip-shaped or knot-shaped Cenci. You can even cut Cenci in the middle and plait the dough passing one of the end through this little hole. Heat abundant oil and deep fry Cenci. Cool and sprinkle with vanilla sugar.

Biscuits in the style of Prato

3 eggs, 3 yolks, 400 g flour, 250 g sugar, 200 g almond, 1 sachet baking powder, salt

Mix two eggs with three more yolks and sugar. Stir in flour gradually and then add salt and baking powder. When all the ingredients combine, add almonds. Almond should have their peel. Stir until almonds are evenly distributed. Knead on a pastry board and form little dough sticks, possibly 1 cm high and 5 cm wide. Place the sticks on a baking sheet. Brush them with yolk and bake at 150°C for 15 minutes. When the surface of these dough sticks is golden, remove them from the oven and cut them into oblique slices. Subsequently, bake biscuits again for 10 minutes. Serve with Vin Santo, in which they can be deliciously dipped

GATTÒ ARETINO
(rolled dessert in the style of Arezzo)

*150 g flour, 50 g potato starch flour, 250 g sugar, 5 eggs,
50 g butter, alkermes, baking powder, salt,
custard cream, dark chocolate, icing sugar.*

Gattò is a traditional dessert of Arezzo. It was the must-have cake for weddings and other celebration. Mix yolks and sugar. Whip up egg whites and add them to the mixture. Stir in a pinch of salt, baking powder, melted butter, flour and potato starch flour. Pour the batter into a rectangular baking-sheet-covered mould. Bake for 15 minutes. When the base is ready, remove it from the oven and wet it with alkermes diluted in water. Dissolve 100g dark chocolate in the custard, whose directions can be found in the recipe of 'Prato Peaches', and spread this double cream on the surface of the cake. Roll the cake avoiding breaking it and sprinkle it with icing sugar.

Rosemary bread

500 g flour, 30g yeast, water, 50 g sugar, 300 g raisin, rosemary, olive oil (800 g bread dough can be used instead of flour and yeast)

Pan di ramerino (rosemary bread) is an ancient recipe which dates back to the Fourteenth century. It used to be prepared in Florence at Easter, especially on Maundy Thursday. Nowadays, it can be easily found in bakeries during Lent. In the past, the availability of this dessert in bakeries was linked with bread, which was baked just once a week. For this reason, these rosemary loaves were available once a week, too. The ancient directions for this recipe were extremely simple: some bread dough was set aside, sweetened with raisin, sugar and rosemary.

Prepare the bread dough three hours before serving the cake. Work sifted flour, yeast, sugar and a glass of lukewarm water on a pastry board. Cover the dough with a kitchen towel and let it stand for one hour at room temperature.

Hydrate the raisin in a bowl containing water. Once the dough has leavened, add drained raisins, a tablespoon of olive oil and rosemary needles. Knead so as the ingredients combine and then form small loaves. Draw a cross on top of each loaf using a knife. Place the loaves into a casserole covered with a baking sheet. Let the bread stand again for half an hour. Brush the loaves with olive oil, sprinkle with sugar and bake for half an hour, until the surface of the bread becomes golden. Rosemary loaves can be served with Vin Santo at the end of a meal. An ancient version suggests rosemary-flavoured olive oil in the bread dough: in this case, avoid frying the oil and remove the rosemary before using the oil.

Ossi di morto
(Italian almond biscuits)

200 g flour, 100 g hazelnuts, 100 g peeled sweet almonds,
300 g sugar, 2 egg whites, 1 lemon (possibly organic)

The name of these biscuits is quite picturesque, as it translates from Italian as "dead man's bones" or "dead man's shinbones". Grind almonds and hazelnuts roughly. Mix them with flour and grated lemon peel in a bowl. Lemon peel is used to give the mixture a good flavour. Beat egg whites until stiff and add them to the mixture. Stir gently until the ingredients combine and the dough is rather firm. Place it on a pastry board and form a long one-cm-wide stick of dough. Cut this dough stick into 7-cm-long "bones". You might as well roll out the dough and cut out round shapes by using a glass. Arrange biscuits in a greased casserole or over a baking sheet and bake at 180°C for half an hour, until biscuits become golden on the surface. Cool and serve.

Ricciarelli

400 g peeled sweet almonds, 400 g sugar, 250 g icing sugar,
vanillin, 2 egg whites, 50 large wafer shapes

Ricciarelli are small Christmas biscuits of Siena. Grind almonds until they form a powder. If you use a mortar, pay attention not to produce oil, as it can easily ooze from the fruits. Mix ground almonds and sugar in a bowl. Add 200 g icing sugar, a pinch of vanillin and stiff egg whites. Stir gently. The result should be a dense mixture. Spoon the batter on the wafer shapes and press it delicately with your hands. You might as well use a knife to give the biscuits a rhomboidal shape, the same they have in bakeries and shops. Place the biscuits on a baking sheet and let them stand for 6 hours. Bake at low heat for 15 minutes. Cool and sprinkle with icing sugar before serving.

Zuccotto

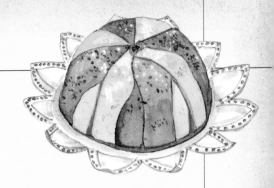

250 g cream, 300 g ricotta cheese, 150 g icing sugar,
250 g sponge-cake, 100 g dark chocolate, 50 g candied cherries and
citron, unsweetened cocoa powder, alkermes (or maraschino cherry
liquor or kirsch), a high-sided hemispherical mould

A Zuccotto is a chilled dessert traditionally prepared in Tuscany. Whip up the cream and add icing sugar to it. Soften ricotta cheese with a fork and combine it with the cream. Divide the mixture into two unequal parts so as one is more abundant then the other. Chop the chocolate and stir it in the most abundant mixture, together with candied fruits. Sprinkle the smallest amount of cream with cocoa powder. Remove sides from the sponge-cake and cut it into strips. Wet the strips with liquor diluted in water and cover the mould. Set aside a few strips. Pour the cream with candied fruits and chocolate flakes into the mould, pressing gently with a spoon. Subsequently, add the cocoa cream and cover the surface of the mould with the remaining strips. Place Zuccotto into the fridge and allow cooling for 5 hours before serving it. To remove zuccotto from its bowl, place a serving dish on top and invert the bowl.

Prato peaches
(peach-shaped pastry in the style of Prato)

Dough: 500 g flour, 100 g sugar, 100 g butter, yeast,
1 lemon (possibly organic), 2 eggs, salt, alkermes
Custard cream: 2 eggs, 150 g sugar, flour, 500 ml milk,
1 lemon (possibly organic), salt

Prato peaches are traditional pastries of Firenze and Pistoia. The dough is given a round shape, wetted with alkermes and garnished with custard cream in the middle. The result is a pastry divided into two halves, coloured in pink thanks to the liquor, which really looks like a peach.

Dissolve yeast in warm water, allowing reactivation. Work eggs, flour, sugar, yeast, melted butter, a pinch of salt, grated lemon peel on a pastry board. Knead until all the ingredients combine and when the dough is ready, cover it with a kitchen towel and let it stand in a warm place for 2 hours. When the time required has passed, sprinkle the pastry board with flour and place the dough on it. Work the dough with your hands in order to obtain balls the size of an egg. Cover them with a kitchen towel and let them rise for one hour more. Meanwhile, prepare the custard cream. Beat two eggs with sugar. Sprinkle the mixture with a tablespoon of sifted flour. Boil the milk with grated lemon peel and pour it in the egg mixture. Cook the batter stirring constantly for 10 minutes. Bake the dough balls for half an hour. When they are ready, remove from the oven, wet each pastry with alkermes diluted in water. Cut each ball into two halves and spread the inside with custard cream. Finally, join the two halves together – cream makes them stick properly – and roll the peach into granulated sugar.

Rice cake in the style of Carrara

100 g rice, 12 eggs, 450 g sugar, 1.2 litre milk, 1 lemon (possibly organic), rum, Strega liquor, vanilla sugar, salt, butter, 28-cm-wide casserole

This is a traditional peasants' dessert, particularly widespread in the area around Massa Carrara.

People used to prepare it at Easter. Rice is not combined with eggs and the cake shows two distinct layers. It is advisable to prepare it in the morning if it has to be served at dinner, or the night before if it has to be served at lunch.

Boil rice in slightly salted water, without overcooking it. Drain, add some sugar so as it does not stick and cool. Boil milk, add 400g of sugar, stir, set aside and allow cooling. Beat the eggs briefly with a fork in a bowl. Add a pinch of salt, grated orange peel and the liquors. Once the milk has cooled, add it to the mixture together with a sachet of vanilla sugar. Greased a mould and sprinkle it with little granulated sugar. Cover the bottom of the mould with rice and then pour the egg mixture very slowly over the rice.

Pre-heat oven at 250°C and bake for one hour, paying attention that the surface of the cake does not become too brown. When ready, cover the cake with yellow paper and cool. Rice cake is usually served cold.

Liquor shots

Livorno punch

sugar, dark rum, coffee, lemon peel

The main ingredients of this drink, which is a version of the English punch, are coffee and liquor. It was first prepared between the Seventeen and the Eighteen century. Not only in the area around Livorno, but also in other Tuscan towns, it is possible to buy it in shops. The most famous brand of Tuscan punch is Vittori, prepared with rum, alcohol and caramel. You can use this Vittori punch as a basis for your Livorno punch, but it is also possible to use dark rum instead. Heat half a shot glass of rum with lemon peel. Add two teaspoons of sugar and an espresso coffee. Stir and serve.
If you have an espresso coffee-maker with a steam

arm, you can use this device to prepare your punch. You might change the recipe a little, in this case. Place two teaspoons of sugar in a shot glass, add the lemon peel, pour the rum and heat the mixture with the steam arm. Immediately afterwards, add a small amount of very hot espresso.

In some bars of Livorno, expert barmen prepare this punch making the coffee float on the liquor. Other possible ways of preparing this punch include other liquors instead of rum: a cognac or a "Sassolino". Tuscan people usually drink this punch after an abundant meal.

Florentine alkermes

350 g alcohol (95 degrees pure alcohol), 350 g sugar, 500 g water,
7 g cinnamon (in sticks), 5 g cochineal (or different colorant),
2 grains clove, 1 g cardamom, 4 g coriander,
1 g nutmeg mace, 1 g vanilla, orange peel,
60 g rose water (for cooking use)

The name of this typical Florentine liquor is derived from the Spanish word "alquermes", which, in turn, comes from the Arabian word "al-qirmiz", whose meaning is "cochineal". This small insect was once dried, reduced to powder and liquors were dyed from it. It gives an intense red colour.
The Alkermes recipe was first written by the monk Cosimo Buccelli in 1743. He was the director of the Officina Profumo Farmaceutica of Santa Maria Novella, a pharmaceutical section of the monastery belonging to this famous church. The original recipe was found in the archives of the Officina.

Nevertheless, it is considered highly probable that Alkermes had been known in Florence much earlier, in the Thirteen century, when the nuns of Santa Maria dei Servi, whose convent dates back to 1233, started to prepare a life elixir of the same colour and characteristics of today's Alkermes. This liquor was very popular by the Medici court and became widespread in France when Caterina de' Medici arrived to the Valois court. Nowadays, original Alkermes is still prepared by the Dominican monks of Santa Maria Novella and sold in the shop near the Church. This liquor and other types of Alkermes sold around Italy do not contain ancient cochineal dye, as they are aromatised hydroalcoholic solutions with synthetic food colourings. We use alkermes to prepare many typical Italian desserts like English soup, Prato peaches, Arezzo gattò, zuccotto, but also Prato mortadella (a type of salted pork).

Grind all the spices, orange peel and cochineal and place the powder into a small jar, together with alcohol and 200g of water. Screw the lid on the jar and let the infusion stand for 15 days. Shake it twice a day. After the infusion period, dissolve sugar in 300g of water and add it to the mixture in

the jar. Let the infusion stand for one more week. Afterwards, strain the mixture and add rose water. Bottle the liquor and wait 30 days before serving.
 If you cannot find natural cochineal, you might as well use synthetic food colourings. In this case, add the colouring after straining the mixture, at the very end of the process. It could also be difficult to find rose water for culinary use, so you can prepare it yourself, by letting some rose petals in a jar containing pure water for 14 days. After this period, strain the rose water and bottle it.

All our books are produced entirely in Italy
using papers from specifically dedicated forestry
operations with regular replanting.
Moreover, all materials used are ecology-compatible
in full respect of the environment and people.
All our production is based on full respect of regulations
concerning safety, consumer health and our workers.

Printed in the month of March 2010
by Editoriale Bortolazzi - Stei
San Giovanni Lupatoto (Vr)